THE PIG WAR
The Last Canada–US Border Conflict

ROSEMARY NEERING

VICTORIA · VANCOUVER · CALGARY

Heritage House Publishing Company Ltd.
www.heritagehouse.ca

Library and Archives Canada Cataloguing in Publication
Neering, Rosemary, 1945–
    The Pig War: the last Canada-US border conflict / Rosemary Neering.

(Amazing stories)
Issued also in electronic format.
ISBN 978-1-926936-01-7

    1. Pig War, Wash., 1859. 2. Boundary disputes—History—19th century. 3. Canada—Boundaries—United States. 4. United States—Boundaries—Canada. 5. Northwest boundary of the United States—History—19th century. 6. Great Britain—Foreign relations—United States. 7. United States—Foreign relations—Great Britain. 8. San Juan Island (Wash.)—History. I. Title. II. Series: Amazing stories (Surrey, B.C.)

F897.S2N44 2011   979.7'7403   C2011-900342-2

Series editor: Lesley Reynolds.
Cover design: Chyla Cardinal. Interior design: Frances Hunter.
Cover photo: English Camp, San Juan Island, May 12, 1868, by Edwin Porcher. Yale Collection of Western Americana 1021844, Beinecke Rare Book and Manuscript Library.

 The interior of this book was printed on 100% post-consumer recycled paper, processed chlorine free and printed with vegetable-based inks.

Heritage House acknowledges the financial support for its publishing program from the Government of Canada through the Canada Book Fund (CBF), Canada Council for the Arts and the province of British Columbia through the British Columbia Arts Council and the Book Publishing Tax Credit.

 Canada Council   Conseil des Arts
for the Arts   du Canada
 BRITISH COLUMBIA
ARTS COUNCIL
 Canadian   Patrimoine
Heritage   canadien

14 13 12 11   1 2 3 4 5
Printed in Canada

Contents

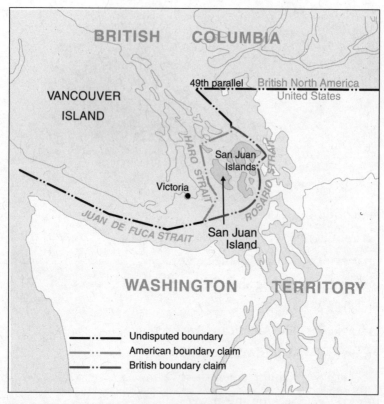

BRITISH COLUMBIA

VANCOUVER
ISLAND

49th parallel British North America
United States

HARO STRAIT

San Juan
Islands

ROSARIO STRAIT

Victoria

JUAN DE FUCA STRAIT

San Juan
Island

WASHINGTON TERRITORY

— ··— Undisputed boundary
— ·—·— American boundary claim
— ·—·— British boundary claim

The San Juan Islands lie between Vancouver Island and the American
mainland. They were claimed by both Britain and the United States.

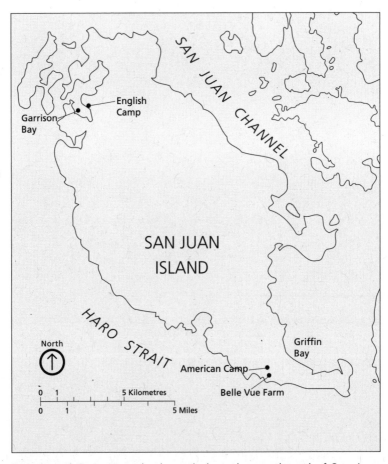

British and Americans both settled on the south end of San Juan Island, the British establishing Belle Vue sheep farm and American settlers their own small farms. The American military fortified their camp at this end of the island; the British later founded English Camp at the north end of the island. US NATIONAL PARK SERVICE

Prologue

IT COULD HAVE BEEN AN *idyllic day on San Juan Island, blue sky over the late-summer gold of the island grasses and the deep green of the trees. Just a few clouds hung above Juan de Fuca Strait, and the silhouettes of the Olympic Mountains showed sharply to the south, with the small town of Victoria just visible on the distant shore to the west.*

Yet the scene in August of 1859 was far from idyllic. On this tiny island far from the centres of power in Britain and the United States, American soldiers settled in behind their heavy field guns positioned high on the ridge overlooking the bay, their deep blue uniforms blending with the undergrowth, their brass buttons glinting in the sunlight. Below the ridge, another 400 Americans marched, wheeled and took part in the daily life of an army camp. Offshore, two British ships rested at anchor, their long guns trained on the American camp. Some 2,000 Royal Marines and British Navy men went about their work, the bright red of the marines' uniforms a sharp contrast to the deep blue and white of the navy.

Meanwhile, in Victoria and in Washington Territory, government officials, military men and newspaper editors threw angry words at each other, demanding that the other side withdraw or face the consequences. These islands at the edge of the United States are ours, announced the Americans. These islands are possessions of Great Britain and have been for decades, responded the British.

Each side declared it would not fire the first shot. But each would respond if fired upon: neither would give way without a fight, for national pride was at stake. As the soldiers, marines and sailors performed the mundane tasks of armies and navies everywhere, day by day, moment by moment, the opposing forces edged closer to war.

Introduction

THE BIG BLACK BOAR SNUFFLED his way through the long grass of the San Juan Island prairie, looking for some tasty tidbits. A Berkshire, a breed well known for rooting, the pig had grunted his way along this path before. He knew something delectable lay ahead, and he wasn't about to be deterred by the ramshackle fence erected by a lazy settler who had enclosed just three sides of his makeshift plot. It was a simple matter to push by the fence, dig his snout into the ground and begin his feast.

The American farmer heard the pig and rushed enraged out of his cabin waving his rifle. One pigly incursion had been an offence, but two, from this same British-owned boar, were a direct insult. Matters were not improved by the presence of a shepherd, a Hawaiian considered by the American to be a black man, who stood by chuckling merrily as the pig gorged himself. The American took aim and blew the pig out of the patch—or, if you believe the other side of the story, followed the pig out of the patch into the woods and shot the miscreant there.

The killing of the pig was the spark that almost set aflame an all-out war between Britain and the United States on the northwest coast of North America. But the standoff on San Juan Island could have been the Sheep War, or the Customs Inspector War, or the You're Too Damned Arrogant War, prompted by a kidnapped flock of sheep, an attempt to collect customs duties, a raid by Natives from far up the coast or the arrest of one man.

The pig was just the catalyst that prompted a much larger event, one of those small incidents that have much larger repercussions. The most infamous of such catalysts occurred in 1914, when the shooting of an archduke by a Serbian nationalist set off four years of bloody war in Europe. But anywhere that hot and hasty men are determined to take umbrage, almost any perceived insult serves to precipitate much larger conflict, and in the 1850s, the northwest had more than its share of such men.

The story of the war that almost was is woven of many a thread of history, warp and woof, British and American. On Vancouver Island and the mainland were the haughty and imperious men of the Hudson's Bay Company (HBC)

Introduction

and the officials empowered by the British Colonial Office, their sense of entitlement fed by two centuries of colonial experience. To the south were the Americans, some a rag-tag bunch of adventurers looking for land, others career army officers spoiling for a fight and officials who believed in America's manifest destiny to rule the continent. Behind the adversaries, a continent and more away, were the leaders and governments of the two nations, opposed to any major conflict in this distant and unimportant region but handicapped by the slow and ponderous communication systems of the day.

The shooting of the pig could have led to a confrontation that saw the deaths or injuries of hundreds or perhaps thousands of soldiers, a completely different American Civil War, a different map of the northwest and a different path in British and Canadian history. Yet this drama played out on a tiny island on the far edge of the continent, a place that few had heard of and even fewer had ever seen.

CHAPTER

1

Setting Up
the Fight

AS JAMES DOUGLAS WALKED HOME across the narrow
white-painted bridge above the tidal mudflats between Fort
Victoria and his James Bay home, his stomach full of good
food and his mind content, he could feel proud of what he
had accomplished. He had risen from relatively humble circumstances to head the mighty Hudson's Bay Company on
the Pacific coast. He held the prestigious jobs of governor
of Vancouver Island and mainland British Columbia. He
headed a large and accomplished family, his house was one
of the best in the colony and he had savings in the bank.

Though some might call him autocratic, he knew without
a doubt that he had saved British Columbia for Britain despite
the territorial ambitions of land-hungry Americans. Though

12

some in the colonies might suggest he ruled with too stern a hand and enforced regulations that harmed commerce, he had kept law and order despite the chaos of the previous year. Though some might call him priggish, laugh behind his back because he was one-eighth coloured and look down on his Metis wife, he treasured his family and encouraged his children. He believed he had treated the Native people firmly but fairly and that he had their respect.

History does not record his thoughts as he strode through the late evening sunshine early in July 1959, returning to his house after dining at the HBC post, as was his custom. But there is much evidence of who he was and what he had done. He had been born 56 years earlier in the South American colony of British Guiana, one of three children of John Douglas' first family, from a long-time liaison between the Scottish trader and a mixed-race "free coloured" Creole woman. He had spent his school years in Scotland, sent there by his father who had returned home, married a Scottish woman and started a second family. He was apprenticed to the fur-trading North West Company (NWC) when he was 16, and headed for British North America. When the NWC merged with the HBC in 1821, he continued on in their employment, rising through the ranks to the position of chief trader at a number of fur forts in the northwest. He had several run-ins with the Carrier people around Fort St. James, and his father-in-law, the chief factor, recommended he be transferred to Fort Vancouver in the south.

"Douglas's life is much exposed among these Carriers," William Connolly wrote to his overseer. "He would readily face a hundred of them, but he does not much like the idea of being assassinated."

Douglas became chief factor at Fort Vancouver in 1839, in charge of the Columbia department and successfully dealing with the Russians to the north and the Natives in his vicinity. But the Americans were another matter. In the 1830s and 1840s, hundreds of American settlers spilled west on the Oregon Trail, looking for free land to homestead. Douglas and his superiors recognized that the influx spelled the end of fur trading in the region, and Douglas was sent out to find a new home for the company. He settled on a pleasant harbour at the south end of Vancouver Island, "a perfect Eden in the midst of the dreary wilderness of the North West coast . . . one might be pardoned for supposing it had dropped from the clouds into its present position." Douglas moved the company headquarters here in 1843, naming the new site Fort Victoria.

The men of the HBC built a palisaded fort and went about their business of fur trading and, to a very minor extent, settlement. Considering it existed on the edge of the wilderness, Fort Victoria was surprisingly genteel. An effete colonial governor came and went, undone by Douglas' firm grip on affairs, and Douglas himself was named governor. Clergymen arrived and departed. A few settlers came to farm, and the company brought in a number of Kanakas—

Hawaiian labourers—to work the farms they established to feed their men. From time to time, a Royal Navy ship put in at the neighbouring harbour of Esquimalt, and officers and men trekked along the muddy trails and roads to dine and perhaps dance at the fort.

Yet, for all the peacefulness of the region, there were clouds on Douglas' horizon.

The Americans are Coming—and Fighting

The Great Migration of 1843 saw some 1,000 people leave the American Midwest for the northern territory west of the Rockies, especially the land along the Columbia River. The wagon trains made their way through the Rockies and Oregon's Blue Mountains. The emigrants cut trail and continued to the Columbia River, where they disassembled the wagons and floated them downriver, moving themselves and their animals along a narrow track near the river. Once a rough road was completed along the Columbia, a wagon road existed all the way from the Missouri River to the Willamette River. Many more settlers would soon follow that road.

The growing settlements were grist for the mill of expansionists who thought the United States should control North America, their nation serving as an exemplar of democracy and a counter to the privileged and tired old nations of Europe. Disputed to this time between Britain and the United States, all Oregon Country should officially become a part of the United States, the expansionists urged, just as they urged adding all of Texas in the south. Their efforts were rewarded by the Oregon Treaty of 1846, which gave the land south of the 49th parallel to the United States. In 1848, Oregon Country was formally declared as Oregon Territory. The arrival of the settlers resulted in conflict with the Natives who lived on the land being claimed, and troops were posted to protect the settlers and make treaties with the Native peoples.

Far to the south, American troops were on the warpath, eventually forcing Mexico to cede a huge territory, including California, New Mexico, Nevada, Utah and parts of Colorado, Arizona, Wyoming and New Mexico in return for a large cash payment (though the payment was about half of what the United States had offered Mexico before the war began).

The US government wasn't looking for more hostilities on its northwestern border, but American citizens moving into the Oregon Territory and American commanders fresh from victory over Mexico were in no mood to bow to any foreign nation.

Gold, Gold, Gold!

Even with the increasing pace of events below the border, life trundled along routinely at Fort Victoria for 15 years. At Fort Connolly in northern British Columbia some years earlier, James Douglas had married Amelia, the half-Cree, half-Scottish daughter of Chief Trader William Connolly.

Now, as their family grew to encompass six children (seven others died at birth or when young), Douglas built an imposing house across the tidal inlet from the fort. Ever a prudent man, he built up his capital and bought more land. His house was filled with books, a piano graced the drawing room and his daughters wore ornate dresses imported from Britain.

Occasionally, troubling events interrupted the generally calm demeanour of the fort. In 1852, American gold seekers who had rushed to the Queen Charlotte Islands when they heard that gold had been found there threatened to set up their own government and take possession of the islands for the United States. Douglas requested help from the Royal Navy, and a ship was sent from the navy's Pacific headquarters in South America. The ship and Douglas' own pronouncements, coupled with the inhospitality of the Queen Charlottes and the relatively small quantity of gold found there, ended the dispute. And, on occasion, Native people erupted into violence, angered at actions of the incomers or looking for loot. When this occurred, Douglas sent men to deal harshly with the people he regarded as the transgressors.

Then, on April 25, 1858, the region changed forever. Throughout the previous year, reports had filtered into Fort Victoria of gold found in the rivers on the mainland. Douglas tried to keep the finds quiet, but this was impossible. Various prospectors came overland to test the sandbars of the

James Douglas, governor of Vancouver Island and long-time associate of the Hudson's Bay Company, was severely tried by the actions of the Americans on San Juan Island and responded with characteristic imperiousness. BC ARCHIVES A-01229

Fraser River, and on that Sunday morning in April, the sidewheel steamer *Commodore* anchored off Victoria after a voyage from San Francisco, and 400 eager gold seekers streamed into the streets of the fort and the tiny town.

Setting Up the Fight

After a few weeks, most had headed out again, by canoe, steamship, even raft, across the Strait of Georgia and up the Fraser. But in their wake came others: more prospectors, merchants, traders, professional men, gamblers, prostitutes, con men and a few families swelled the town. Even a group of black settlers, driven out of California by the anti-black attitudes that prevailed in San Francisco, arrived to settle in Victoria. By summer, the tents, shacks and sturdier buildings newly thrown up were filled with 3,000 residents.

To Douglas' dismay, most were Americans. The governor had good reason to distrust such men. To his way of thinking, the HBC had been unfairly tossed from the Oregon Territory after American settlers arrived. Dispossessed of its rich fur region, with much of the company property taken away, the HBC had been forced to find a new home on Vancouver Island. If he did not act fast, Douglas could see much the same thing happening there.

He decided to wield a firm hand and enforce a strong policy. Even though he had no actual power on the mainland, he declared Crown control over that region and asserted that any incoming miners must obtain licences from him or his representatives. At the same time, he requested military help in case the miners resisted his control. A few months later, he received the news that the British government had created the Crown colony of British Columbia and appointed him as its governor. Now he had the power to back up his pronouncements.

Two navy ships, in the region at the time, came to his aid. The corvette HMS *Satellite* and the surveying vessel HMS *Plumper* were being used in a survey of the neighbouring San Juan Islands. *Satellite* took up position at the mouth of the Fraser; later that summer, *Plumper* joined her. The crews were weakened, though, when one in ten men aboard *Satellite* succumbed to gold fever and hastened upriver themselves.

Over the next few months, some 10,000 men thronged to the Fraser. "Never, perhaps," wrote English immigrant Alfred Waddington, "was there so large an immigration in so short a space into so small a place." The British government, concerned about maintaining order in the region, directed Rear Admiral R. Lambert Baynes, in charge of the Royal Navy's Pacific command, to send assistance.

The British then dispatched the frigate *Tribune*, commanded by Captain Geoffrey Phipps Hornby, and two corvettes from their station in Asia. In addition, they sent the admiral himself, aboard HMS *Ganges*, to the navy base at Esquimalt. By the end of 1858, five navy ships were based at Vancouver Island.

Whose Islands Are They?

When called upon to present themselves at the mouth of the Fraser in the summer of 1858, the crews of *Plumper* and *Satellite* were nosing their ships into the myriad small bays, coves and straits of the islands to the south of

Vancouver Island, trying to chart this complex coastline. Their presence was the result of a poorly phrased sentence in the Oregon Treaty.

In 1846, Britain and the United States settled the question of how to divide the vast Oregon Country. The British wanted the border to follow the Columbia River. Many Americans thought the border should follow the 54°40' line of latitude that marked the southern end of the Alaska Panhandle and of Russian possessions in North America. Imbued with the spirit of manifest destiny, they demanded that the British abandon all their claims to the northwest.

The diplomats came to a compromise. The border would follow the 49th parallel of latitude from the Rocky Mountains to the sea. The southern end of Vancouver Island lies below the 49th parallel, tucked into an open-mouth shape of land, the lower jaw formed by the Olympic Peninsula on the southern side of Juan de Fuca Strait, the open upper jaw by the mainland along the sounds and straits that lead from Juan de Fuca. The treaty declared that Vancouver Island would remain British and that the sea boundary would be drawn from the 49th parallel on the mainland across the open jaw to the centre of Juan de Fuca Strait, then through the centre of the strait to open ocean:

> From the point on the forty-ninth parallel of latitude where the boundary laid down . . . terminates, the line of boundary . . . shall be continued westward along the said forty-ninth parallel

of north latitude to the middle of the channel which separates the continent from Vancouver's Island; and thence southerly through the middle of said channel, and of Fuca's Straits to the Pacific Ocean; provided however that the navigation of such channel and Straits south of the forty-ninth parallel of north latitude remain free and open to both parties.

The formal language of the treaty hid a major problem. On the mainland, things were clear enough. And the boundary path through the middle of Juan de Fuca Strait could scarcely be disputed. But the line that joined the two was dim indeed. There were several channels separating the continent from Vancouver Island. Positioned between these channels were a cluster of islands known as the San Juans. The treaty could be interpreted to mean the correct channel would be Rosario Strait, along the southern side of the San Juans, an archipelago of four major and a score of smaller islands. But it could also be Haro Strait, along the northern side of the islands, or even smaller straits between San Juan Island, the largest of the cluster, and most of the rest of the islands.

The HBC men, probably the most knowledgeable about the lay of the coastline, were dismayed by the lack of precision and begged that the treaty be made more precise, with the boundary specified as Rosario Strait. But the functionaries in the foreign offices knew little and were less concerned. Maps of the region were inadequate and unclear, but the officials considered the treaty language good enough.

Spurred on by the ambiguity, both nations claimed the San Juan Islands. If the borderline was to run through Haro Strait, the islands would belong to the United States. If the border was to be Rosario Strait, then the islands would be British. And if the decision was made for the smaller straits, San Juan Island would belong to the British, while the other main islands would be American.

And then the confrontations began.

CHAPTER

2

Feeling Sheepish

THE MOON AND STARS SHED faint light on San Juan Island on a March night in 1855. The crunch of boat keels on a stony beach broke the silence. Seven Americans climbed from the boats to the shore and quietly made their way up the gentle hill toward the top of the ridge that ran along the centre of the island.

Below them, on the far side of the ridge, they espied several hundred sheep that lay sleeping. The men emerged from the shadows. In the near darkness, they threw themselves on the startled rams that were penned together. Bleats echoed over the grassland as the men lifted and dragged the 220-pound rams back toward their landing place. Each successive capture was more difficult as the nervous sheep bolted in erratic flight.

By dawn, the men had somehow managed to haul 34 rams from the meadows to the shore. There, they had built a pen of logs and branches, and they began to auction the animals. They sold the ones they had captured, and a dozen more that were still at large, for a dollar or 50 cents each, mainly to themselves. Then they prepared to take the sheep back to the mainland and their own farms.

But they had not planned well: there were more captured sheep than would fit in their boats. They commandeered a canoe from a nearby Native encampment and tried to load the rams on board the four boats. But small boats— especially canoes—and struggling sheep are a poor mix. The canoe tipped, the rams butted and several took to their woolly heels.

As the Americans tied some of the sheep into the boats and tried to recapture the other wandering beasts, they looked up to see a dozen men rushing toward them. Alerted by the noise or by someone who saw the Americans stealing the sheep, Kanaka (Hawaiian) shepherds employed by the HBC, owners of Belle Vue, the island sheep farm, had come to foil the plot. The Kanakas—later described by the Americans as armed with knives—opened the makeshift pen and released the remaining animals.

Charles Griffin, manager of Belle Vue farm, came over the hill next. He had been in his house when he "received by the hands of an Indian boy, a note from one of my men, hurriedly stating that . . . these parties had sold the most valuable part of my whole stock, the breeding Rams. 49 in all, 34 of which they had taken away, the remaining 15 were in the Park, which on my arrival here I immediately set at liberty, beside these . . . they sold unseen 24 other sheep, to be taken I imagine by stealth."

The Americans pushed their boats out into the waves. Griffin and a helper waded out into the water and tried to untie the rams and urge them over the gunwales. "These men all armed approached and three of them pushed us off. On renewing our efforts, one of them drew from his belt a Revolver Pistol, which the moment I saw I expostulated with them, telling them I could not possibly contend against such a Force."

The company men retreated, and the boats drew away, the sheep still bleating and struggling in the bows.

It sounds like a comic opera, but the men involved were in deadly earnest. The sheep-napping was part of the larger drama as Americans and British argued over control and ownership of the San Juan Islands.

The Islands Are Ours! No, They're OURS!

The drama had begun in the 1840s. When James Douglas established Fort Victoria, the islands were still primarily the territory of Native bands that camped along their shores or lived in small villages, sustained by fish, shellfish and land and sea mammals. Vexed by the banishment of the HBC from the Columbia River post, Douglas was determined that the British would lose no more territory in the northwest through a failure to establish their rightful claim. The San Juans were perhaps not as strategically or economically important as the Columbia River region, but they did overlook the strait across from Victoria and could be of military importance. Douglas was convinced that the islands were rightfully British, and he did not plan to lose them to the United States through neglect.

In July of 1845, or so he claimed, Douglas sent men south to place a tablet claiming San Juan Island for Britain at the top of a low mountain on the south end of that island. Since the act took place before the Oregon Treaty of 1846 was signed, he declared, San Juan was clearly a British possession.

Did he in fact do this before 1846? Only he and his men knew. But in any case, Douglas doubted that a tablet on a mountain would be enough to keep the Americans away. For several decades, the HBC had been salting and packing salmon at Fort Langley on the Fraser River, for shipment overseas. In 1851, he established a seasonal salting station on San Juan, at the same time taking formal possession of the islands for the British.

But actual right of possession might depend on year-round settlement. And it seemed clear that the Americans were paying more attention to their northwest territories. Many more Americans poured into Oregon after the treaty was signed, and in 1853, the territory was split in two, with the northern region becoming Washington Territory.

The US government dispatched Isaac Stevens to govern the new region. Combat tough, twice cited for gallantry and recovered from serious wounds he suffered in the Mexican-American War, the 34-year-old Stevens was no cautious diplomat. He dealt fiercely with the Native people of the region, threatening and coercing them into signing treaties and sending his troops to subdue them when he deemed it necessary or expedient. He was unlikely to bow meekly to British claims.

Whether or not he was aware of Stevens' reputation, Douglas knew he had to continue to prove the British claim. Though few settlers had crossed the water to the San Juans, an American had cut timber on Lopez Island and was shipping it to the mainland. Not allowed without a permit, Douglas declared, and assessed the American a fee. The American refused to pay but left the island.

Yet it would be impossible to continue to enforce British claims from the safety of Fort Victoria. A greater British presence was required on the islands. Because the HBC had discouraged settlement around Fort Victoria—settlers and the fur trade were not a successful mix—he had few people to spare for the San Juans. The company had already established several farms around the fort, however, to supply its employees and their families and to sell produce to the Russians farther north. The open prairies and grasslands of San Juan seemed ideal for grazing sheep. In 1853, Douglas established Belle Vue sheep farm on the southern end of the island and appointed Charles Griffin to run it. In the dark, rainy days of December, Griffin and some of the Kanaka labourers transported more than a thousand sheep to the island and began building shelters and barns.

According to Customs
Within a few months, a tidy square of a half-dozen white-painted buildings was complete, and sheep grazed in meadows all along the island, the grazings linked by a trail some 15 miles long. As winter turned to spring, the Kanakas cleared and tilled land, planting vegetables and grain around the small settlement. Pigs rooted nearby, and chickens roosted in the hen houses. A few cattle and horses were shipped to the farm.

It didn't take long for American authorities to react to these incursions on an island they considered their own property. Washington Territory had based a customs collector, Isaac Ebey, in Port Townsend, across Juan de Fuca Strait on the mainland. Ebey asserted that the San Juans were American territory, and that he would seize property from the British if they did not pay the appropriate customs duties on all their livestock and possessions imported to the island. Douglas was not impressed. In turn, he appointed Charles Griffin as British Justice of the Peace on the island and instructed him that if Ebey arrived to collect customs duties, he would be breaking the law and should be treated accordingly.

How to emphasize Britain's claim to the San Juan Islands? In 1853, James Douglas sent men and sheep to San Juan Island to establish Belle Vue Farm on the island's natural pastures. US NATIONAL PARK SERVICE

Ebey duly arrived on April 21, 1854, and handed Griffin a bill. Griffin ignored it. Ebey left, but then returned. Griffin sent a message to Fort Victoria, asking for help. "There is a report," he wrote in his farm journal, "that the Americans have left Nisqually on two open boats well manned etc to seize the company's property on the Island here. The *Otter* [an HBC steamer] remains a few days as guard ship." Douglas hastened to Belle Vue but decided not to inflame matters by landing. He sent British customs inspector James Sangster ashore, and Sangster ran a British flag up the farm flagpole. Ebey declared he would land his own resident customs collector. Griffin and Sangster said the man would be arrested if he arrived. Ebey was undeterred: that's just fine, he said, and you had better treat him well when you take him back to Victoria.

Feeling Sheepish

The next day, Ebey appointed Henry Webber as customs inspector. Webber pitched a tent near the farm and hoisted an American flag. Griffin issued a warrant for Webber's arrest and sent a newly named constable, probably one of the farm Kanakas, to arrest the American.

Webber was having none of it. "[He] instantaneously presented a revolver at the breast of the constable, telling him if he touched him he would most certainly fire . . . and if he or any other man or men attempted to arrest him, he should fire, and otherwise protect himself as long as a ball remained in any of his pistols; he had two brace of pistols hung about his waste and breast and a knife thrust in his boot at the knee," ran a report of the British Foreign Office.

The constable withdrew for the moment but returned with a posse of men. "The Constable then called on six men to assist him, but on his going up to seize Webber he presented a revolver in his face, and said if he put a hand on him he would fire, the men demanded arms, and on being refused by Justice Griffin retired. The arms Webber had on him were 4 six barreled revolvers and a large knife in his boot," reported Griffin. Discretion seemed called for. Douglas told Griffin to leave things as they were, unless Webber actually tried to enforce any American laws. Webber desisted, and he and Griffin managed to get along together quite well.

This was not a long-term solution for either side. Communication in the 1850s was slow and difficult, and messages took months to move between Victoria and Britain and between Port Townsend, the territorial capital Olympia, and Washington, DC. Eventually, though, the British Foreign Office heard the duelling customs tale and sent a protest off to Washington. The Americans reassured the British that a joint boundary commission would consider the issue of the San Juans. As far as they were concerned, however, the islands were American territory. And as far as the British were concerned, the islands were theirs.

We'll Do As We Please

Frontiersmen, men of action buoyed by American success in the Spanish-American War, the Americans in Washington Territory were unlikely to be deterred by the niceties of diplomatic negotiation. Possession would indeed be nine-tenths of the law, and they intended to have possession. In 1854, the Washington Territory authorities declared that the San Juan Islands were a part of Whatcom County, which borders the straits and bays of the northwest coast below the 49th parallel.

There were, however, few settlers on the islands. A handful of Americans had come to homestead and farm, but most were frightened away by the tales of marauding Natives sweeping down from the north coast in their massive canoes, raiding settlements, Native and white, all along the coast. While history suggests that most raids on white settlements in the islands were conducted by Native people from American territory, the stories of the northern Natives were fear-inducing indeed. The settlers who remained had to appeal to the men of the HBC for protection, since the Americans had no force of their own in the islands, and the farms were distant from each other and difficult to protect.

Some settlers had taken up land in mainland Whatcom County, and no one was going to tell them what to do. They decided to elect a county government of their own. Newly elected commissioner William Cullen, an Irish immigrant with no love for the English, turned his eyes on San Juan Island and decided it should be part of his domain. The British must pay up or get out. He sent a sheriff, Ellis Barnes, to demand payment of taxes and duties; failing that, a tax sale would be held, he declared, to recoup lost taxes of $80.33. Griffin told him to forget it. The sheriff came to San Juan to auction off some HBC sheep, but no buyers appeared. He went back home.

But Cullen and Barnes weren't through. On that night in March of 1855, they and other Whatcom County residents came ashore to round up as many rams as they could, regardless of the actual taxes "owed," and sell them off to themselves, a good way to get breeding rams cheaply and, in their eyes, lawfully. Despite the efforts of the HBC men and their own blunders, they were able to get more than 30 rams back home with them. Interestingly, in recounting his adventures, one of the sheep-nappers compared himself to a very British hero, underlining the common heritage of Americans and British alike: "We were all worn out from loss of sleep and hard work, the tide was running against us, our boats were heavily loaded, but we bent to the oars and like Wellington at Waterloo, prayed for night or Blucher to come to our relief." (Field Marshall Gebhard von Blücher saved the day for the British forces under Wellington against Napoleon at Waterloo.)

Shorn of his sheep, Griffin took ship for Victoria to report the night's events to Douglas. In his best high dudgeon, Douglas sent a vigorous complaint to Governor Stevens, then dispatched an official complaint to London. London filed a claim for some 3,000 pounds in damages— about $15,000. They didn't get the money, but British protests did not go unheard. The American Secretary of State wrote to Stevens, telling him to back off and have his officials do likewise; until a decision was reached between the nations on ownership of the islands, neither side had the right to push the other around.

At the same time, the Americans were nosing around the islands, checking out their military value. Two US Army topographical engineers arrived in the summer of 1855 and reported back that Haro Strait was, to them, the only logical place for the boundary. The San Juans would indeed have military usefulness, since they provided a good landlocked harbour for refuge that could be easily defended and that would command the approach to American territory. Too bad, they continued, that "no system of defense can be complete without the possession of Vancouver [Island]."

Feeling Sheepish

The situation needed clarity. After 10 years of doing nothing much, the two governments agreed to set up a commission to survey and mark the boundary and make recommendations in areas where the line between the two countries was in dispute. Archibald Campbell was named the American boundary commissioner, Captain James Prevost the British commissioner. The boundary commission, manned on the British side between the Rockies and the Pacific by a newly arrived detachment of Royal Engineers, was soon at work surveying and marking the land boundary. The water boundary would not be as clear-cut.

Prevost was told—in orders not to be revealed to the Americans—to safeguard Vancouver Island as much as possible and therefore to push for Rosario Strait as the boundary. If that could not be secured, then the middle strait through the islands was much the British preference. Both countries saw the possession of San Juan Island as important for the defence of their respective territories. The Americans wanted to overlook Juan de Fuca Strait, so they would have an equal ability with Britain to command that important waterway. Britain did not want the Americans to have that power.

The surveying of the waters and coastline proceeded, but the issue remained deadlocked. Prevost and Campbell met several times in 1857, with each commissioner unsurprisingly hewing to his nation's position. The issue remained unresolved through 1858 and the beginning of 1859.

Meanwhile, on the island, shepherds, magistrates and customs collectors continued in an uneasy truce. James Douglas reported in January of 1857, "The sheep at San Juan are divided into four flocks, kept at as many different stations; each flock being under the charge of an engaged servant, with 3 Indians, and Murdoch McLeod, a very trusted Lewis man, acts as head shepherd. There being no grass or other food for the sheep in the wooded Districts, the sheep stations are, from necessity, placed in the natural prairies of the Island; which are distant from each other, and connected by roads, opened with much labour, through the forest."

The truce would not remain unbroken for long.

CHAPTER

3

The Pig

FIND A PLACE ON THE sandbar where no one else could push you aside. Pull your shovel out of your pack. Fill your gold pan with river gravel. Swirl it in the fast-running river water until all the lighter sand and gravel slide away with the current. There, in the bottom, are the tiny glittering specks that you travelled thousands of miles to find: gold.

If you were lucky. If you were not, your trip via train and rough track, ship and shank's mare, was in vain. Frustrated and dirty, at night you retired to the blind pig, drank execrable whisky and maybe fought a few rounds with another disappointed man or lost what little money you had to a con man or card shark.

For hundreds, the Fraser River gold rush meant success: gold dust or even nuggets secreted in a pouch and taken back downriver to be evaluated at the assay office or simply sold to a buyer. For the successful miners, the journey from San Francisco or from the east coast of the United States or Canada was worthwhile. For the card sharks and gamblers, the easy women and merchants, the rush was equally profitable. But for thousands, the Fraser River was the big humbug. Many would-be miners arrived while the river was still high and ran out of money before it dropped, or they got there after the best sandbars had been staked. Others were just unlucky. Clergyman Matthew Macfie, who arrived at Victoria in 1859, wrote:

> Individuals of every Trade and profession in San Francisco and several parts of Oregon, threw up their employments, in many cases sold their property at an immense sacrifice, and repaired to the new *Dorado*. This motley throng included, too, gamblers, "loafers," thieves, and ruffians, with not a few of a higher moral grade. The rich came to speculate, and the poor in the hope of quickly becoming rich . . . Several thousands, undismayed by the dangers and hardships incident to crossing the gulf and ascending the river, proceeded to the source of the gold.

But, noted Macfie, they were ignorant of the rise and fall of the river, and their patience or their provisions were soon exhausted:

A gloomy impression began to prevail among the less venture-some spirits that tarried in this field of morbid speculation. Gold not coming down fast enough to satisfy their wishes, thousands of them lost heart and went back to San Francisco, heaping execrations upon the country and everything else that was English; and placing the reported existence of gold in the same category as the South Sea bubble.

Macfie noted that the great majority of the men who flocked to the Fraser and to Victoria were American, and many were hostile to British control of the area, in part because Douglas had forced all would-be miners to get licences and had enforced British law upon the rowdier elements. Macfie describes one reaction:

The "rowdy" element had assembled [in Victoria], finding no legitimate occupation to employ their idle hands, and were under strong temptation to create such disturbances as they had been accustomed to get up to in California. Losing, for the moment, that wholesome dread of British rule which that class usually feel, a party of them rescued a prisoner from the hands of the police, and actually proposed to hoist the American flag over the old Hudson's Bay Company's fort. But the news that a gunboat was on her way from Esquimalt to quell the riot, soon calmed alarm and restored peace.

Though many Americans simply returned whence they had come, some had no desire—and some had no money— to go back home. And some were eager to find a piece of land where they could homestead. Those who decided to stay in the region, but who were not keen on remaining in British territory, looked south of the 49th parallel. Some 20 to 30 men decided to stake claims on San Juan Island. A number of these men were southerners, who regarded both the Kanaka shepherds and the Native people as inferior beings, even though several of them lived and had children with Native women. Most were fiercely independent frontiersmen who brooked no government interference in their lives.

They were not a good mix with the men of the HBC, who tended to be suspicious of democracy and autocratic with Americans. And Douglas was still utterly determined that San Juan Island was and would remain British. When new settlers arrived in 1859, bringing with them a surveyor whose job was to lay out lot lines in preparation for land claims, Douglas was disturbed. "There is little doubt," he wrote, "that the whole Island will soon be occupied by a squatter population . . . if they do not receive a check . . . [But] I fear that Her Majesty's Government would not approve of my adopting measures for the summary and forcible ejection of squatters." At the same time, though, "circumstances may call for decisive action." Kick the squatters out, he said to his superiors in London, until the boundary has been settled. If necessary, send in troops to evict the settlers. Until he received instructions, though, Douglas feared his hands were tied.

The Pig

One of the disappointed goldrushers who hied to San Juan was Lyman Cutlar, a tall, fair-haired frontiersman who wandered the West seeking his fortune after he left his Kentucky home. Now in his mid-twenties, Cutlar was a restless soul, averse to authority and determined to live where and how he pleased. An independent American, described by one source as "one of the unwashed sovereigns of the United States who did not scare worth a cent," he was unlikely to bow to British authority. A southerner, he did not acknowledge blacks or Natives as equals, though he did have a Native wife and child.

No one is quite sure how or when Cutlar arrived on San Juan Island. Quite probably he heard about the island from other Americans as he made his way south along the mainland. Considering any British claims to the island to be invalid, he settled on a piece of land near Belle Vue headquarters, built a log shanty and moved in with his Native companion. Legend has it that he rowed across to Port Townsend for a sack of seed potatoes, which he planted near this cabin. Never known as a particularly hard worker or good farmer, he built a makeshift fence that partially enclosed his garden.

Griffin was not happy about Cutlar's presence or that of the other settlers. He claimed they interfered with the sheep runs, which was indisputable, since they built their cabins in the middle of the runs and made life difficult for the herdsmen. They even brought cattle to the island and let them graze on the HBC sheep pastures. But, instructed not to get

41

in their way or do anything to interfere with them, Griffin could only suffer their presence in relative silence.

Until May 15, 1859. By then, the HBC had on San Juan some 4,500 sheep, 40 cattle, 5 yoke of oxen, 35 horses and 40 pigs, among them prized Berkshire boars that had sired much of the sounder.

For several centuries, the Berkshire breed had been the favoured hog for the British upper-class landowner. Large, black and producing meat of excellent quality and flavour, weighing up to a thousand pounds at maturity, the Berkshire was imported to America and Canada from England early in the 19th century and bred with American hogs to produce sterling beasts. But the Berkshire had a less admirable side: the boars, especially, rooted extremely well and frequently in mud and dirt for whatever food they could find, and they were stubborn and cantankerous, not easily moved from their chosen path.

The Berkshire boar that wandered from the Belle Vue barns to the potato patch of Lyman Cutlar had worked his way into the patch on a previous occasion, and Cutlar had threatened to shoot the beast if he returned. "Keep your pig out of my potatoes," Cutlar is said to have declared to Griffin. "It's up to you to keep your potatoes out of my pig," was the purported response.

Early on May 15, Cutlar awoke to the sound of someone's laughter. Bursting from his cabin, he discovered a Kanaka herdsman leaning against a tree and chuckling as the boar rooted through his potatoes. He saw the hog "at his old game," Cutlar later wrote. "I immediately became enraged at the independance of the negro knowing as he did my previous loss and upon the impulse of the moment seazed my rifle and shot the hog." Was the pig still in the potatoes when he shot it or had it moved to the forest? Did Cutlar's anger at the man he called a "negro," a "nigger" and "colard" fire his rage as much as the actions of the pig? Accounts differ, but the result is in no doubt. Cutlar fired and the boar fell dead.

His sense of satisfaction at having bested his enemy was soon tempered by a sense of fairness. He walked the two miles to Griffin's house and offered to pay for the dead pig. Fine, said Griffin: $100 please. Cutlar's temper flared again. Surely the pig was worth no more than five dollars, ten at the outside. He replied, "I think there is a better chance for lightning to strike than for you to get one hundred dollars for that hog." The argument escalated into a battle over whether Cutlar and his fellow settlers had any right at all to live on the island. Griffin threatened to have them removed; Cutlar replied that they had a perfect right to live on American territory, which this was.

Griffin wrote immediately to Douglas. He was concerned about more than the shooting of the pig. Cutlar had "used the most insulting & threatening language & openly declared he would shoot my cattle if they trespassed near his place." Unless something was done about Cutlar, he told Douglas, not only would Griffin be in danger but so would his herdsmen. "This same man told me to my face he would as soon shoot me as he would a hog if I trespassed on his claim." Griffin hadn't backed down. "I distinctly gave him to understand he had not a shadow of a right to squat on the Island much less in the center of the most valuable sheep run I have on the island." Cutlar had answered back, wrote Griffin, that American authorities had told him he was on American soil and that he had the right to claim land there and live there.

There were now more than 16 squatters on the island, said Griffin, and they were all building and farming on the sheep runs. "One of them only a few days ago landed upwards of 20 head of Cattle . . . & has frequently said that the Surveyor General of Washington Territory had distinctly told him that as soon as a few American citizens were once settled here on the island he would have the place properly surveyed."

The next day, three officials visited: the head of the HBC in the region now that Douglas had resigned, another HBC functionary and a member of the Vancouver Island Legislative Council—a nice mix of company and civil interests. The visit was possibly coincidental or might have been a result of the report of the pig shooting and the subsequent quarrel. The three visitors went with Griffin to Cutlar's cabin. Cutlar later wrote that the foursome threatened him, saying that if he did not pay the $100, he would be arrested and transported to Victoria for trial. Cutlar, in turn, replied that they'd better bring a posse, for he and his friends would fight any such move with whatever force was required.

The Victoria men reported the discussion very differently. They had, they said, merely dropped in upon Cutlar to continue the discussion over the boar, whereupon Cutlar had threatened to shoot any other HBC animal that encroached on the American's claim. "I remonstrated with him in regard to his offense which he admitted offering to pay the value of the animal killed, which was not accepted," wrote Alexander Dallas, HBC area chief. "No demand of $100 or any sum of money was made upon him, nor did I threaten to apprehend him or take him to Victoria. On the contrary I stated distinctly that I was a private individual and could not interfere with him." This is what Dallas should have said, since he had no powers of arrest.

What was the truth? Probably it lies somewhere between the two accounts. But Cutlar told his side of the story to American customs inspector Paul Hubbs Jr., another southerner, who had been posted on San Juan Island. Hubbs, who was easily outraged, had already complained to his boss about the "intolerable and odious" monopoly exercised by the HBC on the island. He was only too pleased to protest this latest affront. Settle the boundary in our favour now, he demanded, or send troops to protect us from these insulting actions of the British. Otherwise, he wrote, American settlers could be kidnapped by the British or the HBC (he made, and there was in fact, little distinction between the two) and "shut up in the prison of the British Colony somewhat worse than Dartmoor was in 1813," referring to Americans imprisoned in a horrendous British jail during the War of 1812. Considering the tiny jail and small community of Victoria at the time, it was a more-than-dubious comparison.

Hubbs, having sent his demands, jumped in his rowboat and headed off to Fort Bellingham, where he spoke to the commander of the fort, Captain George Pickett.

Back on the island, all the American settlers were spoiling for a fight. The Fourth of July was rapidly approaching. What better event could there be than a flag-raising to underline the American claim to the island and put those arrogant Britishers in their place? Fourteen Americans met on their national holiday at Hubbs' cabin, not far from Belle Vue headquarters, and made fiery anti-British speeches. Up went the 55-foot flagpole, its rising marked by volleys of shots.

Griffin promptly raised the British flag on a pole above his own house.

4

The Americans
Are Coming

ON JULY 9, AMERICAN GENERAL William Selby Harney crossed Juan de Fuca Strait aboard USS *Massachusetts,* after a courtesy visit to Victoria and Governor James Douglas, and arrived at San Juan Island. Harney, the commander of the American military in the Department of Oregon, was making a tour of settlements in the area and was undoubtedly pleased to see the American flag flying high above the island.

Harney disembarked, then walked through the HBC settlement to Hubbs' house, accompanied by the excitable collector of customs. Hubbs described in graphic terms the settlers' fear of the northern Natives, claiming against all truth that the HBC let them raid American settlements and kill Americans at will, an interesting judgment considering the settlers had previously commended the men of the HBC for protecting them against Native raids. Then he described the killing of the pig and the succeeding events. We are powerless here, he said to Harney. Send troops to protect us.

A few days later, after Harney's departure and perhaps at his behest, Hubbs submitted a petition signed by 22 American settlers on San Juan, asking that soldiers be sent to protect them from the Native people.

The petition was heeded. Much to Hubbs' satisfaction, Captain Pickett was ordered from his post at Fort Bellingham to San Juan Island. *Massachusetts* was to convey the soldiers to San Juan and then patrol the surrounding channels, to be ready in case of any further quarrels with the British and to prevent Native raids.

Harney had a more grandiose mission in mind than the mere protection of the settlers on San Juan. He wrote to the commander of the American army to tell him of his actions and reported that since Britain had not colonized Vancouver Island, "this, with pressing necessities of our commerce on this coast, will induce them to yield, eventually, Vancouver's Island to our government. It is as important to the Pacific States as Cuba is to those on the Atlantic." San Juan, meanwhile, had a commanding position over the surrounding waters. It also had timber, good water and grass, the best harbour for a naval station on the Pacific coast and was a good place from which to observe the northern Natives and prevent any possible raids.

On July 26, after dark, Pickett landed on the beach near Hubbs' cabin. The two met and decided the army camp would be built a stone's throw from the HBC wharf. The next morning, Pickett landed his company of 60 men and began to make camp.

On an island with a variety of suitable harbours and campsites, Pickett's choice was provocative. It was logical enough, since the dock provided an excellent landing place for men and supplies and a strategic site in the face of any British response, but it was also very much in the face of the HBC and James Douglas. Though he was supposedly on the island to protect Americans from the Native people, he chose to post a proclamation that seemed intended to inflame Douglas and his compatriots. "This being United States Territory," it read, "no laws other than those of the United States, nor courts, except such are held by virtue of said laws, will be recognized or allowed on this island." Why such an inflammatory notice? Some see a plot by him and Harney; some just see bad judgment.

Whatever the reasons, the act was in character for both Harney and Pickett. In later correspondence, Harney reported half-truths as facts, complained bitterly of British arrogance, said the HBC representatives were using British naval ships to further the company's ends and declared that "any attempt at possession [of the island] by them will be followed by a collision." Though he later withdrew most of his falsehoods, the damage had been done.

Harney and Pickett

Name a military action involving the United States between 1818 and 1860, and William Selby Harney was there. Born in Tennessee in 1800, he joined the US Army when he was 17 years old. He was there when the US military forced infamous pirate and smuggler Jean Lafitte out of his base of operations in the Gulf of Mexico. He fought in the Blackhawk War against Native nations of the Midwest and in the First Seminole War in Florida; one biography describes him as developing "successful techniques to hunt the Seminoles." When the Mexican-American War broke out in 1846, Harney was fighting Comanches in Texas. He immediately enlisted a force of volunteers from the American settlers in the region, crossed the border and occupied the small border town of Presidio, all without orders. He had been given some discretion to act, but the invasion was too much for his superior officers, and they ordered him back into the United States immediately. But Harney was in no hurry to comply; it took him five days to retreat. His actions demonstrated "extreme imbecility and manifest incapacity," wrote his commanding officer.

It was not Harney's first brush with army officialdom, or his first hasty and foolish action. Fighting the Indian Wars, he was reckless with the men under his command and vengeful with Native Americans. "He has no more brains than a Greyhound," wrote another army officer. "By his stupidity ... he had done more to inject the Indians with

Without William Selby Harney, would there have been a Pig War? The American army officer's fondness for combat and confrontation heightened the tensions on San Juan Island.

a fear of us . . . than all the other commanders." He was known among the Sioux as "the woman killer." Yet others considered him a fine officer, and he was promoted to colonel during the Mexican-American War and to general shortly thereafter. When he was reprimanded for his fecklessness, US President James Polk, a fellow Tennessean, commended him as one of the "most gallant and best officers in the service."

The red-haired six-footer was a commanding figure, distrustful of any authority other than his own. "I'm for battle not for peace," he said, and his career prospered. Placed in charge of Oregon Territory military, Harney tried to court-martial other officers in Washington Territory who challenged his authority, and he obeyed only those orders that he agreed with. He was bound to come into contact with the British, whom he had been taught to hate by a patron in his early army days.

Virginia-born Captain George S. Pickett was another colourful character. A popular cadet and the class clown at West Point military academy, he graduated last in his class in 1846. But the army, newly embroiled in Mexico, needed officers, and Pickett was duly commissioned. Some foolishly brave acts attracted attention, and he served in Texas before being posted to Washington Territory, where he was placed in charge of building Fort Bellingham.

The British Respond

The British and Americans were now in a state of high dudgeon, ready to see insults to their nation's honour in even the smallest act. The truth was often the first victim, as each side and each participant spun the story to reflect their own views.

Not surprisingly, the British were outraged at the proclamation posted by Pickett declaring that San Juan was indisputably American territory. The first to read the notice was John DeCourcy, the newly appointed British Justice of the Peace on San Juan. Dispatched to the island by Douglas, DeCourcy was instructed to evict the American squatters from HBC land and arrest the trespassers, granting bail to make sure that they actually attended their trials in Victoria. He was also told not to do anything that might lead to acts of violence. It is difficult to see how he could have accomplished his first instruction without breaching the second.

On his arrival, DeCourcy immediately confronted Pickett, asking him by what right he had occupied the island. Pickett said he was commanded to do so by his superior officer. DeCourcy ordered Pickett to leave the island. Pickett refused and introduced DeCourcy to the American magistrate, who told DeCourcy the British had no authority on the island.

The opposing sides were at a stalemate.

Riff-Raff and Whisky, Navy and Threats

An army is said to march on its stomach, but camp followers pay close attention to other parts of the body as well. As soon as Pickett and his troops landed, the riff-raff of the west coast followed. They set up a village not far from the American camp and sold liquor from tents or from shacks that they towed to San Juan from an abandoned mining camp in Bellingham Bay. Prostitutes, most of them young

Native girls, were the next arrivals. Soon the muddy main street was thronged with settlers, sutlers, soldiers and salesmen. The reporter from the *Victoria Gazette* dropped by and regaled his readers with a description of the result. "Some three or four persons had started little groggeries near the landing from the harbor and several parties had been in a state of drunkenness the night before," he noted. And Charles Griffin bemoaned the fact that "Soldiers, Inds & Men all been determined to be drink together. Never saw anything like it."

Many of Victoria's residents wanted to see what was going on, and the Victoria–San Juan route became a regular picnic run. In the week or so after the troop landing, some 500 people sailed over to check out the American camp and the HBC sheep station, and, presumably, to take refreshments.

Soon after the American troops landed, HMS *Satellite*, the ship that had brought DeCourcy to the island, sailed for Victoria to take the news of the landing to James Douglas. But the morning paper had already broken the unwelcome news. "We trust our government will call our insatiable neighbor to account for the unwarrantable assumption" that the San Juans were American, raged *British Colonist* editor Amor De Cosmos. The "clandestine landing" of American troops was "so unwise and unpolitic a step," he huffed. "Like thieves in the night, they sought to plant themselves on an island over which we have exercised sovereignty many years, and to which . . . we are lawfully entitled."

De Cosmos' interpretation of the Oregon Treaty and British rights in the region perhaps overstated the case. But there was no doubt that the landing of American troops on San Juan was a significant escalation in the battle over the island. While men on both sides of the question did call for forbearance and diplomacy, others shouted for vengeance over the perceived slight to national honour. Both sides publicly declared they would not fire the first shot, but neither would they submit tamely to a forcible takeover. The Americans declared that if the British fired the first shot, they would fight against the British until the last American soldier had been killed or captured.

James Douglas was in a quandary, one caused partly by his dual loyalties. For most of his adult life, he had served the HBC, and his loyalty to that company was strong. When he was named governor of British Columbia, however, he had to give up his company position and work solely for the Crown. Yet the interests of Crown and company were intertwined on San Juan Island. He was bound by duty and a strong desire to protect British interests on San Juan, but the only British on the island were the HBC men and the civil magistrates he had placed there. And it was clear that the Americans viewed company and Crown as one and the same and were equally resentful of both.

Could Douglas order British troops to the island, in part to protect commercial interests? It had been done before and would be done again in other parts of the colonial empire.

But Douglas needed firmer ground to stand on; he needed instructions from his masters in London.

It would take a long time for those instructions to arrive. A trans-Atlantic telegraph was still five years in the future. There were no transcontinental rail lines in either British North America or the United States. Douglas sent off a request for advice, but his letter would take some six weeks to get to London. Ironically, it would have to pass through American territory, by ship to San Francisco, then again by sea to Panama, overland to the Caribbean, then by sea to Britain. Alternatively, and questionably, given that the Americans were rapidly becoming the enemy, his missive could travel by trail and rail across the United States, then by ship from New York to Britain. A reply would take an equal six weeks to reach Victoria. It was now late July. He could not expect to get an answer to his questions before October.

Douglas needed to proceed on his own. He could be diplomatic, but it was not in him to back down or be subservient to the Americans. The first imperative, he thought, was to show the flag in a way that could not possibly be misinterpreted. Since he had requested Royal Navy help in dealing with the influx of gold miners the year before, five navy ships were docked at Esquimalt or at sea along the northwest coast. Could he send one of these ships to San Juan?

Rear Admiral R. Lambert Baynes, commander of the navy in the Pacific, was away at his other base in South America. In Baynes' absence, Douglas was in temporary command of the navy ships in the northwest waters. He ordered the 31-gun Royal Navy frigate *Tribune* to San Juan Island and instructed its captain to prevent any further landings by American soldiers. He was also told to prevent the troops that had already landed from fortifying any part of the island. He was, however, not to use force to carry out his orders. Faced with British naval might, conjectured Douglas, the Americans would surely turn tail and run.

On July 29, Captain Geoffrey Phipps Hornby sailed *Tribune* into Griffin Bay on San Juan Island. He went to meet Pickett, but the American captain was away from camp. With relief, Hornby noted that the American camp was very lightly fortified, so he would not need to confront the Americans immediately. Nevertheless, he decided, it would be very difficult to winkle the Americans out of their camp. They were unlikely to leave willingly, so it would undoubtedly require armed force to move them. And even if he were successful, what would happen next? He was trapped by conflicting orders. He was to tell Pickett to leave, but he was not to force him to leave. If he did have to fire on Pickett's camp, the Americans were unlikely to submit tamely just because the British had more men and more guns. They would instead dispatch more troops from their Fort Bellingham headquarters. The confrontation would escalate; soldiers and sailors would die or be injured. Was the situation worth a war between the two countries? Was there no other path?

Anxious August

On July 30, Hornby sent a message back to Douglas via the HBC steamer *Beaver*, while the government officials Douglas had sent along on *Tribune* reported that the American forces were stronger than expected. Fine then, said Douglas, we'll show more strength ourselves. He ordered HMS *Pylades* to San Juan Island. But Michael DeCourcy, the captain of that ship, was not prepared to go. Escalating the dispute, he thought, would only make things worse. DeCourcy knew Douglas was temporarily in charge of the Royal Navy ships at Esquimalt, but he did not want to move without the approval of his actual boss, Rear Admiral Baynes.

Instead of immediately setting sail, DeCourcy and Captain George Richards of *Plumper* met with Douglas. Richards asked Douglas for more specific instructions; he was understandably confused by orders to make the Americans back up without using force. Perhaps, suggested Richards, the boundary commissioners could meet and work out a way to cool the quarrel. Reluctantly, Douglas agreed to suspend the warrant for Pickett's arrest. He also cancelled Hornby's order to land British troops as necessary. But he still wanted to let the Americans know that they were not in for an easy time. He dispatched *Plumper* to Griffin Bay with an instruction to pick up marines and Royal Engineers from New Westminster, in case British troops needed to go ashore to face American troops.

Pickett, meanwhile, prepared to make his stand. He had

moved his camp from its original site near the HBC wharf, where it was under the guns of navy ships standing off in Griffin Bay, to a site on the other side of the peninsula, not far from Griffin's headquarters. He was well aware, however, that the British could fire on him from Juan de Fuca Strait and could rapidly summon enough men to destroy his camp and drive his men into the woods. But he would never surrender. If forced to fight, he said, the Americans would make a "regular Bunker Hill of it," referring to the famed battle between British soldiers and American rebels during the Revolutionary War in 1775. Or perhaps he didn't say this at all: the quote was reported years later in a highly coloured account of the events of the day. Whatever he may have said, Pickett now took stock of his own position and decided his troops would be better located elsewhere.

Even so, he and his men would still be outmanned and outgunned. Pickett wrote to Lieutenant Colonel Silas Casey, the man in charge of the troops at Port Townsend, asking that *Massachusetts* return to protect the American troops. "It is not comfortable to be lying within range of a couple of war steamers," he told Casey. "The *Tribune!*, a 30-gun frigate, is lying broadside to our camp and from present indications, everything leads me to suppose that they will attempt to prevent my carrying out my instructions."

Tribune was a steam frigate, a battleship that carried a full complement of sails but able to use its 200-horse-power, coal-powered engines to manoeuvre so that its

31 guns could be brought to bear on installations on shore. USS *Massachusetts* was less impressive: a steamer that was used to move troops and supplies around the area, it carried only eight long cannons that fired 32-pound ammunition with a range of 2,000 yards. But it would at least make Pickett feel a little less helpless and exposed on shore.

The following day, the new orders reached Hornby just before he met and talked with Pickett. He was to remain anchored in Griffin Bay and avoid a collision at all costs. In a letter to his wife, he wrote that it was good Pickett had been absent on the previous day. "I have not the disgust of having blustered, and then been obliged to haul in my horns."

That same weekend, Amor De Cosmos decided to have a close-up look at the San Juan situation. Ever fond of the journalist's prerogative of making friendly reports from the enemy camp while firing hostile broadsides from his editorial columns, he sailed over to San Juan aboard a private ship. Faced with adverse tides and winds, it took him two days to cross the strait.

He described the HBC sheep station with its six small dwellings, the hundred or so cultivated acres around the station and the general lay of the land. "A herd of 4,000 and odd sheep, with some 1,900 lambs were quietly grazing below" the ridge. As he moved around the south end of the island, his visit became something of a travel junket. He told his readers:

The first thing that particularly attracted our attention was a small Union Jack flying near Mr. Griffin's house, the H.B. Co's agent, and a few rods further on was a large and new flagstaff, surmounted by the Stars and Stripes. Near it in a small house lives Mr. Hubbs ... On passing, he kindly invited us in to partake of his hospitality, of which we shall always retain a pleasing recollection.

Mr. Hubbs was rapidly packing up his books, preparatory to a sudden removal. Hot and hasty words had passed between Captain Hornby, of the H.M.S. *Tribune*, and Captain Pickett, of the United States forces, and a collision was immediately expected.

Suitably refreshed, De Cosmos continued on to Pickett's camp. "On entering the camp, we were very politely and hospitably received by R. Craig, surgeon to the forces, who invited us to be seated within his marquee. Refreshments being served, we passed a quarter of an hour very pleasantly in his company, and Mr. Crosby's. Mr. C is the American magistrate." De Cosmos' party continued on, taking yet more refreshments with Captain Pickett. "Then we parted, feeling sorry that the occasion had called these gallant men to visit our soil on other than the most friendly terms." Friendly everyone might be, but De Cosmos was in no doubt about whose soil he was standing on.

In fact, De Cosmos noted, if San Juan was ceded to the Americans, "it would afford an excellent shelter in time of war, and prove dangerous to our commerce." Then, cleverly riding two horses at once, he stated that if the Americans did not do as they were told by the British, "it was feared that a collision would follow—which might unfortunately plunge the two greatest nations on earth into bloody war, that would set civilization back half a century." Nonetheless, he continued, it was up to the Americans to give way to prevent this cataclysm. If they did not willingly give way, they must be forced to do so by "the naval forces at our command . . . We are lawfully entitled to it [the island] by occupation and treaty. To relinquish it would be a national crime."

De Cosmos' report appeared in the Monday, August 1, edition of the *Colonist*. That same day, a correspondent who described himself as "a native and continuous Yankee" made the trip to San Juan on behalf of the rival Victoria newspaper, the *Gazette*. Captain Pickett being away, the correspondent was received by another American officer "with that frank hospitality which characterizes the profession in all civilized countries." Several officers from the British ship *Tribune* were seated "in front of the marquee. I was very glad to see this, not only because it justified my preconceived opinion of the gallantry and generous character of British officers, but because it nullifies the acts and assertions of a class whose only aim at present seems to be to engender feelings of animosity between two great nations." He blamed Douglas and his previous loyalty to the HBC for this animosity.

And yet the *Gazette* correspondent quoted Pickett's

inflammatory posting at the camp that San Juan was US territory. He referred to a rumour that Douglas had ordered the arrest of the American officers. "A party from town circulated a report that if the soldiers *were* interfered with, the Americans of Victoria would burn the town. I am glad to know it was not an American or a present sympathizer with Americans who started such a story so insulting to American character, and devoid alike of magnanimity and truth," he continued, blithely spreading a rumour without naming the source, while at the same time condemning those who would spread such a rumour. Everything would be fine, he suggested, "unless patriotism outruns discretion, and insatiable feelings of jealousy or hatred urge on to dishonorable war." Fortunately, the brave and cautious Captain Pickett was in charge of the American troops.

Hornby, meanwhile, was telling his wife in a letter that Harney was undoubtedly making his move because one day he hoped to become president of the United States.

August 1 was an eventful day. *Massachusetts* arrived at Griffin Bay with some 120 additional troops aboard. Contemporary and later accounts are confusing, but it seems clear that army captain Granville Haller did not land those troops. He did offer to put them on land, but he also told Pickett that he was treading on treacherous ground. Pickett should know that it was Harney's agenda he was following, not any orders issued by the American government. Harney, said Haller, was causing trouble for his own reasons, and Pickett should be aware of this. Later that day, *Massachusetts* departed.

Pickett continued moving his camp. James Prevost, the British boundary commissioner, had been looking for Archibald Campbell, in the hopes of finding out what was going on, but the American commissioner was nowhere to be found. Instead, Prevost talked to Pickett, reminding him that the islands were in dispute between the two nations. They are, though, said Prevost, undoubtedly British. Pickett was less aggressive with Prevost than he had been with other British representatives but still declared the islands were American. Prevost returned to Victoria.

In that town, both the officers of the HBC and government officials were increasingly concerned. Alexander Dallas wrote that he understood that the Americans were absolutely determined to resist any landing of British troops. "If this be true bloodshed will inevitably follow and a flame be raised that will not be easily quenched."

The Legislative Assembly of Vancouver Island now weighed in with its opinions. This elected assembly, established in 1856, had little real power, except to approve the spending of government funds. Only a small number of Victoria's residents could vote to elect the assembly, and most of the voters had connections with the HBC. In addition, Douglas chose whomever he wanted as members of the government and could still appoint the members of the Legislative Council, the executive body of the government.

Yet both assembly and council could make noise, and the council decided it was time to do so.

Together with James Douglas it sent an emissary off to England, via San Francisco aboard *Pylades,* to inform the Colonial Office about the brazen invasion of British territory. At the same time as it condemned the American action, it wanted no armed conflict. It decided that the British magistrate should leave the island, and that British troops should not be landed.

Douglas was not convinced. If the Americans were staying, then the British should have an equal force on shore, he wrote to Hornby on August 2, the same day that *Plumper* arrived at Griffin Bay with 46 marines and 15 Royal Engineers from New Westminster. At the same time, Douglas told Hornby that he relied on the latter's discretion. If Pickett was recalcitrant, he said, "The sin will rest upon their own heads." He was reluctant to provoke a battle, but he was determined that no British subject would be harmed, and no sacrifice would be made of British honour and dignity. A joint occupation was the only answer. And he sent along a formal protest that Hornby was to deliver to the Americans.

Hornby was still understandably concerned that his new instructions would end in combat. *Satellite* had returned to Griffin Bay with Prevost aboard, so Hornby, Prevost and Richards set out across the island to meet with Pickett. The meeting solved nothing. Hornby gave the formal protest to Pickett and declared Britain had the right to do anything that the United States did on the island, including landing equal troops and having its own magistrate. Perhaps, he said, a joint military occupation would be the best solution. Pickett asked for time to get new orders from Harney. Hornby grew weary of the indecision and warned Pickett he must accept the occupation or bear the consequences. Pickett did not challenge the British, but his anger was clear in the dispatch he sent to Harney, giving details of the British presence and asking that *Massachusetts* return to Griffin Bay.

Pickett wrote, "I had to deal with three Captains, and I thought it better to take the brunt of it. They have a force much superior to mine that it will be merely a mouthful for them; still I have informed them that I am here by the order of my Commanding General, and will maintain my position as far as possible." The British wanted a joint occupation, he wrote, but he had declined anything of the sort. He had used the utmost courtesy and delicacy in the meeting; perhaps Harney could tell him if a joint occupancy would indeed be possible, so that a collision could be prevented.

Hornby reported back to Douglas. "His [Pickett's] orders as a Soldier gave him no discretion but to seize a small force; to attack an equal one; or to protect against the advance of a superior." Hornby, in turn, had told Pickett that he would land British troops if "the honor of the Flag, or the protection of our rights as subjects demanded it."

The stage was set for conflict. Would August bring war?

5

Words, Words, Words

AS ARMY AND NAVY OFFICERS, governors and boundary commissioners tried to find their way through the dispute, they were urged on to action by the fourth estate. When prospectors or settlers rushed into a region in the West, the man with the printing presses was rarely far behind. A traveller who was writing a book or reporting back to a faraway newspaper was always eager to find new experiences to titillate his readers. And peace doesn't play nearly as well as conflict in the news and editorial columns.

The Olympia *Pioneer and Democrat* began publication in 1853, the year before the creation of Washington Territory. Strongly pro-American and expansionist, it echoed in its columns the land-hungry claims of incoming settlers. The poem entitled "Frazer River," published by the paper on November 5, 1858, succinctly expressed its views on American expansion north of the 49th parallel:

Up above, among the mountains,
Men have found the golden fountains;
Seen where they flow! Oh, joy transcendent!
Down, down, in noiseless stream transplendent,
Then, hurrah, and set your riggings—
Sail above, to richer diggings.

When news gets where Buck and Cass is,
Johnny Bull can go where grass is,
He may rave and rant to foaming,
It will never stop our coming.
Then, hurrah, nor wait for papers,
The license men may cut their capers.

Soon our banner will be streaming,
Soon the eagle will be screaming,
And the lion—see it cowers,
Hurrah, bossy, the river's ours,
Then hurrah, nor wait for calling,
For the Frazer's River's falling.

One of the most colourful of the western newspapermen was the aforementioned Amor De Cosmos, lover of the world, who had changed his name from plain old William Smith. De Cosmos cranked up a hand press to deliver the first issue of Victoria's *British Colonist* on December 11, 1858. We intend to be, he thundered in this first issue, "an independent paper, the organ of no clique nor party—a true index of public opinion. In our National politics we shall ever foster that loyalty which is due to the parent government, and determinedly oppose every influence tending to undermine or subvert the existing connection between the colonies and the mother country."

Yet De Cosmos was no admirer of James Douglas. In his first issue, he denounced the governor and lamented the opportunities he had missed. "He would have been the most popular man in these colonies. His life would have been honored; his death lamented, and his name imperishable." But no, sorrowed De Cosmos. By mixing together the interests of the HBC and of the British government and the colony itself, Douglas had behaved shabbily. When it came to the San Juan crisis, there was little doubt that De Cosmos would be pro-British yet anti-Douglas.

De Cosmos erupted on July 27, as the American troops landed: "We trust our government will call our insatiable neighbor to account for the unwarranted assumption [that San Juan is American territory]. The first thing that will follow will be duties and taxes imposed by the United States and Washington Territory, and on British subjects, who may reside there, and serious disputes may grow out of it. When the title of the island is definitely settled in their favor, it will be time to allow Americans to quietly garrison the island, and not before."

The *Gazette*, on the other hand, was very much pro-American, which was not surprising as it was run by three California newspapermen who had arrived from San Francisco in the summer of 1858. While the editors paid all due respect—how much that was they did not say—to the British element in Victoria, the *Gazette* opined that Vancouver Island and the mainland required American immigrants, since those recently arrived from Britain did not seem to have the character traits required to develop a new country. What would it matter, asked the newspaper, if the islands were simply ceded to the United States? Provided the ports remained open to commerce from Vancouver Island, there would be no problems. James Douglas had no authority to land troops on what the editors called Bellevue Island, presumably for the British sheep farm thereon. And, said the editors on July 30, "there can be little doubt that ultimately the possession of the island will be adjudged to the United States—such being clearly the fair interpretation of the treaty."

The *Colonist* took the *Gazette* to task for its pro-American stance. A letter writer expressed his ire at some of the comments printed in the *Gazette*. "Being an Englishman and living in a British colony, I naturally expect the press . . . to be ready at all times to uphold the rights and dignity of England as a nation," he wrote, shocked and appalled that the *Gazette*, which surprisingly he called a government organ, was approving of the American action of landing troops on San Juan, purportedly to protect the settlers against the Natives. "Now I was not aware that the island was of such dimension, and the outrages of the Indians so numerous and bloody, as to call for a force of several hundred soldiers as a safeguard."

Little concerned about the appropriateness of the comparison, he said the treachery of the *Gazette* could be compared to that of the brute fiend who had stabbed a helpless girl on a Victoria bridge. "That an English editor of a British journal . . . should assume a position so inimical to the country, whose Queen he owed allegiance and where he is earning his daily bread."

Across the border, the Puget Sound *Herald* began publication in 1858. To the south, the San Francisco papers were always happy to comment on Pacific Northwest affairs. Various correspondents reported to the *New York Times* and the London *Times*, and the Toronto *Globe* reprinted articles from the Victoria and American press.

As ever, the newspapers' editorial columns indulged in the usual "shoulda, coulda, woulda" judgments on political actions. But in those more jingoistic days, they were quick to urge action and condemn lack of action when it came to the interests of their respective countries. Outrage, pride, outraged pride and injured honour played a large part in many of their communications.

American writers were just as florid as Victoria ones. The editor of the Puget Sound *Herald* wrote on August 5:

One of the cubs of the old British lion has wandered some thousands of miles from home, had his toes trodden on, the other day, and thereupon set up a terrible howling. Having had an extensive domain set apart for his use, which was generously given him by his neighbor, he now seeks to possess the domain adjacent, and howls when his neighbor places his foot upon it, as though he were treading on the cub's corns. This is but natural. The more one gives the more one is expected to give; and just in proportion as one gives liberally is the giver rewarded with ingratitude.

A fearful tempest is raging in the minds of Her British Majesty's most loyal subjects in British Columbia, just now, because the American authorities have deemed it advisable, for the better protection of American property, to place a garrison on an island that rightfully belongs to them, and which right, we doubt not, will be admitted and conceded by all intelligent and liberal Englishmen.

The concessions made through the Oregon Treaty seem insufficient, said the editor, to "satisfy the greedy maw of John Bull." The writer gave an approving nod to the *Victoria Gazette* for its accurate and fair portrayal of the incident. The newspaper's views were based on its absolute certainty that the island belonged to the United States. "No American officer can for a moment admit it as a disputed territory," declared the editor in a September editorial.

The *New York Times* republished a letter first published in the Philadelphia *Public Ledger* from Paul K. Hubbs Sr., father of the American customs collector on San Juan. American authorities had, said Hubbs, dreadfully neglected the American settlers on San Juan, who were in constant danger of being butchered by Natives from the "northern territory." He added, "So far as San Juan Island was concerned, we had *no protection from death for one hour* but in the moral aid and strong arm of the Hudson Bay Company." Hubbs went on to describe the killing of the pig:

> The boar making appropriation of a potato patch, which the aforesaid settler deemed necessary to his own stomach, took issue with the boar as to the right of property; finally shot the boar, and immediately went to the chief factor of the Company, stated frankly what he had done, and asked to pay for the boar. Now I knew that same old boar; and he certainly was a great "boar," but rather elderly. I have no doubt the Company's gentlemanly agent, Mr. Griffin, would have sold, *on other occasions*, that same old boar for five or ten dollars, the price of young ones in the country, but the "insult to the Hudson Bay Company" required an addition of $90, and $100 was asked, not in the "usual gentlemanly manner" of the agent aforesaid.

Hubbs continued, in language colourful and colloquial, to describe the confrontation between the agents from Victoria and Cutlar, and the subsequent events. "No one intelligent believed the British government capable if truly advised, of committing the follies that have occurred," he concluded.

The London *Times* published a number of articles on

the Pig War, most of them necessarily weeks after the fact.
In September, a report sent from San Francisco in mid-
August described the San Juan rumours swirling around
San Francisco. A correspondent babbled:

> We have an exciting rumor this morning to the effect that the
> British war steamer *Satellite* had bombarded the United States
> military station recently established upon San Juan Island.
> The story comes in a roundabout way, and is probably false.
> We received the intelligence through a telegraphic dispatch
> from Yreka, a town in the extreme northern part of California,
> just over the line from Oregon. A messenger arrived at Yreka
> yesterday from Portland Oregon, with dispatches from Gen.
> Harney to Gen. Clarke, at San Francisco, supposed to be in
> relation to the San Juan Island difficulties. Just as the messenger
> was leaving Portland for Yreka, the rumor above noticed gained
> currency, with the additional rumor that the *Satellite* had fired
> shot and shell, killing upwards of thirty Americans.

The messenger said he could get no positive information,
as he was compelled to leave at once with the dispatches
for General Clarke. The correspondent noted that
steamers frequently plied the Puget Sound waters and that
information could be sent from Olympia to Portland in a
day. If the British had fired, he said, General Harney would
undoubtedly have let people know by now.

At times, American, Canadian and British newspapers
took a measured, non-jingoistic view of the affair, reprinting

each others' articles regardless of whether they originated north or south of the border. The Toronto *Globe* reprinted an October 4 *New York Times* report on the events on San Juan, judging that General Harney's conduct was appalling:

> General Harney is severely condemned by the most intelligent and educated of our countrymen on the spot for this action [ordering American troops to offer armed resistance to any landing by the British], on the ground that no matter how clear and indisputable may be our title to the island, as long as it is a subject of controversy or correspondence between the two governments, *it is disputed territory*, and neither party has a right to sole and exclusive occupancy or jurisdiction over it ... We are indebted to the forbearance and magnanimity of the English naval officer for the continued peace between the two countries, as Gov. Douglas, of British Columbia, ranking as Vice-Admiral, had decided to land the troops. Admiral Baynes, commanding the British fleet, opportunely arrived, countermanded Douglas' insane order, and hence our continued peaceful relations.

The same correspondent had a snide comment on Harney:

> Gen. Harney, who is here called "Goliath," for two reasons—first, that he is a very large man; and second, that he is all matter and no mind—ought, I think, to be court-martialed, and dismissed from the service for his conduct in this case ... The man is not half so fit to be a general as to be a hostler of a livery stable ... Things looked very dark here for a while and war seemed inevitable. We must thank God for the opportune arrival of the English admiral.

The article may have been penned by American army captain Lewis Hunt, who heartily disliked Harney and whom Harney heartily disliked. It was probably Hunt, or possibly another officer, who also said in a letter to the newspaper that Harney was "one of the weakest officers and most arrogant humbugs in the army and not at all qualified for his position. He is a laughingstock, wherever he goes; and his administration is a series of blunders and mistakes." All the officers on San Juan denied writing the articles.

The strong words of writers and editorialists in Washington Territory and Victoria, encouraging war though piously pleading for peace, put pressure on the military and civil authorities to stand their ground and preserve their nation's honour. The next steps in the dare-you dance waltzed the two countries even closer to war.

6

Reinforcements Arrive

BY THE END OF THE first week in August 1859, Britain and the United States were linked in an uneasy confrontation, the British mostly on Royal Navy ships, the Americans on land. No one wanted to be the first to fire a shot in anger. No one would turn the other cheek if the other side fired first.

On August 4, Rear Admiral R. Lambert Baynes returned to the northern seas. First to spy him was *Pylades* captain Michael DeCourcy. Beaten back by weather on its run to San Francisco, *Pylades* was sailing north when DeCourcy saw the flagship of the Royal Navy in the Pacific, the old sailing ship HMS *Ganges*, with Baynes aboard. DeCourcy lowered a boat and battled across the waves to tell his commander what was going on.

The officer commanding the Royal Navy fleet in the Pacific, Baynes had entered the navy in 1810, when he was just 14 years old. By 1855, he was a much-decorated and respected officer. In that year, he was promoted to rear admiral; two years later, he was given charge of the Royal Navy in the Pacific, headquartered in Valparaiso, Chile. Unimpressive physically, short, balding and calm, with a Scotsman's self-deprecating sense of humour, he was straightforward and definite in speech.

In 1858, Baynes was instructed to respond to Douglas' plea for assistance in managing the prospectors' rush to the British Columbia goldfields, helping to maintain law and order and provide a strong British presence in the northwest. In October of that year, he arrived at Esquimalt aboard *Ganges*. Noting that all was quiet since most of the miners had left for the winter, he left in November for Callao, Peru, and Valparaiso, sailing north again the next summer, completely unaware of the debacle on San Juan.

Baynes docked at Esquimalt on August 5, suitably astonished by the behaviour of both American and British sides in the dispute. Ever the calm head in a storm, he is reputed to have said, mildly, "Tut, tut, no, the damn fools," as he took over leadership of the naval forces from Douglas. A week later, he cancelled orders from Douglas to land troops and issued commands confirming Hornby's decisions to keep the British marines and sailors on board ship.

"Avoid all interference" with American soldiers, he

told Hornby. "By every means in your power . . . prevent the risk, of collision taking place." Hornby was not even to assist John DeCourcy, the civil magistrate sent to San Juan by Douglas, unless absolutely necessary. Douglas was to tell DeCourcy not to interfere with American settlers or troops. Since the British could easily land if they chose to, their forbearance would serve them well: there would be no insult to the British Crown and no diminishing of the British position.

Douglas smarted under Baynes' decisions. Hornby had disobeyed Douglas' direct orders, and now Baynes was reinforcing Hornby's position. Hornby, too, was a little bitter, especially when British sources credited the headstrong Douglas with keeping the peace. "That is rather good," he wrote to his wife, "when one knows that he would hear of nothing but shooting them all at first and that, after all, peace was only preserved by my not complying with his wishes, as I felt he was all wrong from the first." Nonetheless, whatever the newspapers wrote and critics in Britain suggested, Hornby got credit where it counted: with Baynes and his fellow officers.

But Baynes' quiet diplomacy raised the ire of the self-designated patriots who bridled at every belligerent action by the Americans. One of the members of the British Columbia House of Assembly was carried away by the eloquence of his own verbosity, as reported in the *British Colonist* of August 17:

A General on his own authority had invaded our territory. His grounds for doing so were based on falsehood and carried out clandestinely. What more could be expected of a man who had spent a life-time warring with the Indians ... Instead of fighting, Her Majesty's captains take to diplomacy ... I am ashamed to think that the Post Captains were holding a pow-wow with a subaltern of the American army. They should have landed their troops and avoided all degrading negotiations ... A militia must be raised. We must defend ourselves, for the position we occupy to-day, would make the iron monument of Wellington weep, and the stony statue of Nelson bend his brow.

Even Douglas, though, had to admit that it was too late for the British to land troops. But if they didn't land troops, what should they do? The present situation could not continue forever, with American soldiers on land and much of the British naval might in the Pacific on battle alert, its commander unable to tend to other duties lest fighting break out once he turned his back.

Baynes suggested that a joint civil occupation might serve the purpose, with both countries withdrawing their forces until the boundary commissioners could make their recommendations and one country or another take over the islands. It was a good idea, but General Harney and Captain Pickett were not interested in returning to that ancient arrangement. Finding common ground would not be simple.

The Americans Double Up

Harney was all too willing to show his mettle. He was under attack from his own men for using soldiers to build himself a private home. He had been termed weak, arrogant and incompetent. Faced with equally strong criticism in the Mexican-American War, he had not hesitated, and in the end, he was praised and his commanding officer denigrated. Criticized equally strongly for his brutal conduct during the Indian Wars, he had continued to behave in the same way. He was not about to change his ways for a mere skirmish in the northwest. If he were able to throw the British off the island without a war, it would be all to his credit and his career would prosper. But if he had to engage in battle against the British and thus win more territory for the United States, he would gain fame and perhaps be propelled into the upper ranks of the army, if not of the nation's government. A man of action, he could see no drawback to his plan.

Please help me, for our troops are much outnumbered, Pickett had written to Harney in early August. With the letter came the official protest penned by James Douglas, claiming that the American occupation was illegal and that the San Juan Islands were British by right of claim that extended well before the American claim. Harney reacted in character. He sent Douglas a letter criticizing him for using a Royal Navy warship to carry out an arrest of an American citizen on behalf of the HBC—even though this had never happened.

He wanted redress, and until he received it, the soldiers would stay on San Juan. He then prepared to up the ante.

Some 500 artillery, infantry and engineer officers and men were billeted to Fort Steilacoom, near the foot of Puget Sound, south of present-day Seattle. They were part of the American military presence in the northwest, sent there primarily to deal with the Natives. Harney ordered Lieutenant Colonel Silas Casey to lead most of these troops to San Juan.

Like Pickett, Casey was a career army officer who had shown no particular distinction in his class at the military academy, graduating 40th of 42. Nonetheless, he served with distinction in the Mexican-American War and was badly wounded in that conflict. He was 52 years old and commander of the district of Puget Sound when he was ordered to San Juan. He was a conciliator whose cool head was much needed on the island.

Harney was an agitator; the word "compromise" was not in his vocabulary. After he ordered Casey to go to San Juan, while Baynes was trying to find a mediated solution to the problem, Harney went on a rampage. He wrote a letter to the War Department, using all the incendiary adjectives he could muster. He called down the HBC for its pretensions, swallowed and regurgitated a highly coloured and virulent account of the pig incident and complained vigorously about the presence of British navy ships. "It would be well," he wrote, "for the British people to know the American people of this coast will never sanction any claim they may assert to any other island in the Puget Sound other than Vancouver's [Island] . . . any attempt at possession by them will be followed by a collision."

The British, he said, were too perfidious to be dealt with amicably. By military means, Harney would maintain the American hold on San Juan. Harney made a number of half-true claims: that the islands were under American control, that foreigners had paid American taxes, that the British had not tried to exercise any rights under their claims and therefore had no extant claim, and that the arrival of the Royal Navy ship was inexcusable. Harney wrote to San Francisco to ask American naval authorities to send ships to reinforce the troops now on Puget Sound, and he posted more men to Fort Steilacoom, putting them at Casey's disposal. He then told Pickett to reject any idea of joint occupation and prevent the British magistrate from exercising any authority over anyone or anything.

While Harney was writing, Casey was moving. He loaded his troops and supplies aboard a sternwheeler. Unaware of the new British orders, Pickett was by now close to panic. He had been chatting with various British officers, and all had been well, but he did not trust the British. News arrived that *Satellite* was on its way to the island; before long, it was near the new American camp. Pickett was convinced it was about to fire on the camp. The fusillade would surely be followed by a full-out assault as men landed from *Tribune* and attacked the Americans from the other side.

Ever more fearful, Pickett sent a message to Casey, delivered by a steamer that chased down Casey and his ship: the British would fire on him if he attempted to land more troops at Griffin Bay. Casey was not convinced that this was true. As his ships sailed cautiously through heavy fog off San Juan, though, he decided it might be better not to test the British resolve. On August 10, he landed his men and their howitzers on a beach some distance from the wharf. Casey continued on to Griffin Bay, where he landed with his army's tents, provisions, ammunition and other supplies. Under their new orders not to interfere with the Americans, the British stood by aboard *Tribune*.

Casey was bemused when he heard Pickett's thoughts. If they were about to attack, why had the British quietly stood by when he landed his supplies and ammunition? But he was new to the island; he did not know the situation and was not ready to argue with Pickett. The forces commanded by Casey and Pickett were dispersed, lined along the hills. The newly arrived howitzers, large cannons that could fire their ammunitions in a curved trajectory, were trundled up the ridge and placed overlooking Griffin Bay. But Casey did not want a battle. If a shot was fired, he would retreat up the island, away from the British guns.

The British refused to co-operate with Pickett's wilder imaginings. Instead, when Casey asked for a talk, Hornby came ashore and the two sat down with boundary commissioners Prevost and Campbell to discuss the situation. When Hornby said his orders came from Baynes, Casey requested a meeting with the rear admiral. Come to Victoria, said Baynes. Casey and Pickett did so, in full uniform. But pride and protocol prevented the meeting. Casey refused to go on board Baynes' ship to meet the British commander; Baynes had no intention of leaving his ship to meet a lower-ranking officer on the vastly inferior American ship. "It is extraordinary," wrote Baynes, well aware of naval etiquette, "that they could have expected me to descend from my position to meet them on board the United States steamer." The British Colonial Office concurred, suggesting that Baynes, who wanted a friendly resolution to the question, was invited "in an insulting manner" to go aboard the small American steamer, in a British port no less. The Americans, army men and less constrained by rank and geography, were not amused. "I was of the opinion," wrote Casey, "that I had carried etiquette far enough in going 25 miles to see a gentleman who was disinclined to come 100 yards to see me." Casey and Pickett retreated to San Juan.

Rebuffed, Casey decided he needed more troops to reinforce the American position. He requested from Harney the other four companies at Fort Steilacoom, plus engineers to build fortifications and heavy guns to defend the camp. Harney was delighted to grant his request.

Douglas now tried to reinsert himself into the negotiations. As governor of the territory, surely he, not Baynes, should have been meeting with Casey. Displeased with Pickett and

Casey for bypassing the civil authority, and a little miffed with Baynes, Douglas wrote to Lord Lytton at the British Colonial Office. The occupation by American troops had, he declared, been undertaken without the knowledge of the American government; surely once the government knew of the actions, it would repudiate them, he declared. He wrote to Harney, denying that the HBC had any control over the islands or influence with the colony's government, challenging Harney's account of the incident involving Lyman Cutlar and denying various other of Harney's charges. If you had a problem, you should have discussed it with me before dispatching troops, he said. Please withdraw your troops now.

Though he was not aware of it, he was getting reinforcement from an unexpected source. American boundary commissioner Campbell was also writing to Harney, for he too had been bypassed in any decision making. Landing more troops, he wrote, could seriously embarrass the United States. Since the matter was under consideration by the boundary commission, the precipitate action could prejudice the American case in any future decision.

Back on San Juan, the two sides were still facing each other, one on land, one at sea. Casey, still unaware that the British were under orders not to engage and suspicious of the British ships with their guns trained on shore, was digging in—literally. He brought in shiploads of lumber to build gun platforms and barracks for his troops. He began to entrench the camp and build a fortification for his heavy guns. He moved

Massachusetts' guns to shore, but left them on the beach since he had no way to move them to more salient positions.

On August 17, four more artillery companies and a military band arrived at Griffin Bay and marched over the ridge to the American camp. The British offered no opposition to the landing of the troops. The American tally now stood at 15 officers, 424 soldiers and another 50 workmen. Standing off in Griffin Bay, the British now counted 3 ships, some 2,000 men—most of them sailors, not fighting soldiers, plus a few hundred marines and Royal Engineers—and 167 ship's guns.

Hornby was not pleased with the arrival of so many more American troops. Even though he had been ordered not to engage in battle, it might yet come to a fight, and he thought the British were being outmanoeuvred. The placement of the howitzers on the ridge made landing any British troops difficult and any attack on the American camp perilous. He wrote to Baynes:

> At first they landed 50 men and professed their object was to protect their citizens, especially from Indians. Now they had 400 soldiers on shore with six (6) Field pieces, eight 32pdr. Mounted, and it is said, six more iron guns under cover in their camp. Six of their heavy guns are placed on the ridge of the hill overlooking the harbour, and by throwing up a parapet, they could command the harbour; even in their present position they would be difficult to silence. The other two heavy guns and field pieces are placed to defend their camp. They seem to me therefore, not only to be prepared to defend themselves but to threaten us.

The British had few fighting men on land in the northwest, but Royal Navy ships called frequently at Esquimalt, across the strait from San Juan Island. The British sent the 21-gun HMS *Satellite* and other ships to show the flag and take any necessary action in the dispute. US NATIONAL PARK SERVICE

And word was that Harney himself was on the way with yet another 400 men. What am I supposed to do, Hornby asked Baynes, if they try to throw the British off the island or tear down our flag? Should I ignore the insult or fire to let them know the British lion can still roar?

Ever the conciliator, Baynes replied that Hornby should not react. If and only if the Americans fired on the British ships should Hornby take any action he thought necessary.

On August 20, the pro-American *Victoria Gazette* urged restraint. "The question . . . can only be complicated by action based on prejudice and passion. The American occupation is an accomplished fact; it cannot be prevented nor recalled by any steps on the part of the British authorities . . . No good can possibly result from measures that will result in a collision, while the harm that will follow is incalculable." If the colonial authorities took hasty action, war would follow before the British government was even aware of the situation.

Now it was the turn of American visitors to drop by the camp. Richard Gholson, the Washington Territory governor, arrived "with several ladies" on board a steamer to review the troops. "The Governor was received by two Aids of Colonel Casey, and a short distance nearer camp by the Colonel in person," reported the *Gazette* on August 27, delighted to have some fancy American news for its columns. "As the party advanced toward camp, a detachment . . . fired a salute of 17 guns, using for the purpose the five 12-pound mountain howitzers comprising the main part of their present field battery, and the nine company were under arms and passed in review upon the broad and grassy plain." Not to be outdone, the officers of HMS *Satellite* invited the governor on board.

But despite official politeness, a compromise seemed as far away as ever. The Americans continued to push their claims, seemingly determined to raise British ire. Customs collector Paul Hubbs Jr. now declared that the ships bringing curious day-trippers from Victoria would have to clear customs at Port Townsend, making a long detour to the south and more than doubling the length of the trip. When John DeCourcy returned from picking up provisions in Victoria, Hubbs stirred the pot again, declaring that DeCourcy would have to pay duties on his shopping, although the Americans who had accompanied him did not. DeCourcy refused. Hubbs blustered. Pickett and Casey wisely stepped in and countermanded Hubbs' order. Peace was restored to a degree, though Hubbs now turned his resentment on Pickett and Casey, angered that his own military had prevented him from asserting American authority.

Relations were friendly enough between the rival military commanders that Casey could attend church services aboard *Satellite* on August 17 and tell his soldiers not to interfere with the Belle Vue Farm livestock and shepherds. Even so, Casey wanted to be prepared for the worst. As the soldiers suffered through wind and rain at their makeshift camp, he decided the site was ill chosen and in a poor strategic location. He moved up the ridge to the slope overlooking Belle Vue Farm and Juan de Fuca Strait and erected conical tents on the site. The guns were dragged up the slope to a position where they could command Griffin Bay.

"I shall put my heavy guns in position to bear on the harbor," Casey wrote, "and also on vessels which might take a position on the other side. Shells from shipping may be able to reach us, and we may not be able to protect the camp from them; but I shall try." The new arrivals plus a team of sappers that arrived on August 23 began fortifying the repositioned camp. "Have platforms made for your heavy guns," were his instructions, "and cover your camp as much as possible by entrenchment, placing your heavy guns in battery on the most exposed approaches . . . select your position with the greatest care to avoid fire from the British ship." The engineers and grunts would build the redoubt using the lumber that the Americans had stockpiled on the beach.

On this team was William Peck, a 25-year-old farm boy from Connecticut who had enlisted in the army as a foot soldier the year before, looking for secure employment and with a desire to see something of the world. Peck kept a diary revealing the life of a military camp, including the tedium of the day-to-day activities and his disappointment with army life. Perhaps few soldiers actively wished for combat, but young men restricted to the day-in, day-out routine of drilling, marching, building, eating and the like might well have desired some excitement to enliven their days.

Peck had already encountered tedium, bad food and miserable conditions while serving at Fort Cascades and other temporary camps in Washington Territory. On August 21, en route to Griffin Bay, he noted that "the representative of John Bull is said to be as ugly, nasty, and mad as our own Harney, and trouble is looked for." But he was sanguine about the expected events, seeing them as a cure for the boredom of life on the outer edge of the American empire. "I am not sure, but with all our humbugging and hardship, it will be a good school for me and I will learn more than I could otherwise have found out." The troops showed some bravado as they landed. As they came ashore, "The men pulled directly under the guns of H.B.M. Sloop of War *Satelite* and the musicians played 'Yankee Doodle' for dear life . . . We are to maintain the honor of the nation and lick the British, no matter the odds brought against us."

In fact, Peck found himself delighted with life on San Juan. The climate was moderate, the scenery delightful and the work not onerous. On a Sunday, he and his fellows went for a wander, saw the famed "white squaw" (presumably, a fair-skinned Native in San Juan village), viewed the Native salmon-drying racks and dropped in on settlers and shepherds. It wasn't all blue skies, however: the troops had not been paid for six months and were very short of the cash required to pay for the delights of the village. Somehow, though, many of the men were able to buy enough whisky to get drunk and often disorderly. If they went too far, they were duly imprisoned, often punished by having to undertake unpleasant work and then released to start their pleasurable round once more.

The sergeant in charge was particularly susceptible to the charms of life in that disreputable village of camp followers. After his first few sprees, he had "recovered his usual irritable equanimity and declares that he will never drink more, but we know that the first towney who comes along will cause him to forego his good resolutions and get drunk." And so it was. "Sergeant McEnaney is drunk [and] disgraced himself again," Peck noted on September 17. "It is extremely fortunate that he is about the worst man in the detachment, otherwise it would be difficult to get along. Invariably, upon going to town he meets some person from his portion of Ireland and comes home drunk . . . so that it is becoming a common subject of ridicule among the men." The men finally received their first pay in eight months on October 14 and 15; not surprisingly, the good sergeant was drunk again by October 17 and again on October 23. He was reduced in rank to first-class private and sentenced to forfeit some of his pay.

Other temptations existed for troops who were single men or far from their families. "There are about 200 Indian women assembled here, almost all of whom are prostitutes, which causes considerable trouble in camp," Peck reported on September 3. "The men absent themselves often, sickness is very prevalent and the discipline of the command is materially injured by their presence." Though no similar diarist existed on board the British ships, it's likely that they were prevented only by their confinement on board ship from enjoying the temptations of shore life quite as much as did the American soldiers.

For the leaders of the two sides, however, life was much more serious.

CHAPTER

7

Seeking an Answer

WHETHER AMERICAN OR BRITISH, the main characters in the San Juans drama were engaged in a peculiar combination of outraged national feeling alternating with courtesy and almost friendship. Washington Territory governor Richard Gholson, for example, was capable of sputtering rage when he thought he was being ignored by the military and not accorded the proper respect in the conduct of affairs, yet he was happy to go aboard *Satellite* when he visited San Juan.

Matthew Macfie, the English clergyman, as British as they come, who described the Fraser River gold rush with such detail, dropped by San Juan in August 1859 on his way to his posting in Victoria. On his way north, Macfie met a US Navy officer who invited him to come along on a trip to

San Juan via the American vessel *Shubrick*, promising they would drop him at Victoria after the visit. He was delighted to accept the invitation and arrived at Griffin Bay in the evening. His description gives a fine picture of the relations between the two supposedly warring nations.

Once the American ship dropped anchor, close by *Satellite*, which, Macfie reported, had its guns "shotted" (loaded and aimed) in the direction of the American camp, a boat from the Royal Navy ship came by to pick up mail that, by necessity, arrived via San Francisco. Mistaking Macfie for the Bishop of Columbia, who was imminently expected, the British then sent a boat to take Macfie under their protection. But by that time, Macfie was on shore, "visiting the enemy's quarters." Once he had seen the American guns and fortifications, Macfie declared that "I am not sure that our nation has ever been so nearly precipitated into war with 'Brother Jonathon' since 1812." Such perceived hostility notwithstanding, Macfie went off to visit the tents of many of the American officers, observing that they were reluctant to be where they were and that they had "none of that thirst for war with England . . . which characterises the less cultivated portion of American citizens." He dropped in on Casey and found him "more concerned, if possible, than his brother officers that harmony should be maintained between the two countries, and assured me he was using all his influence on the side of peace. He regarded it, he said, as the greatest calamity that could befall the cause of civilisation all over the world, that two nations, allied by community of race, language, laws, and religion should be plunged into hostilities. This was saying a great deal for a man whose fortune was war."

But Casey was at pains to reiterate to Macfie that his fine feelings would not apply if a shot were fired. "'It is almost certain,' said he, 'that in that case your ships would blow our handful of men here to atoms, but 300,000 men would instantly pour in from the states and take our places.'" Then Casey asked Macfie to come back as soon as he could to conduct religious services for the men, an American minister presumably not being resident in San Juan village.

Macfie blamed the standoff largely on Governor Douglas' prejudice against and dislike of Americans. If it were not for Hornby and Baynes, wrote Macfie, war would have been inevitable. Unaware of Harney's belligerence, he put much of the blame on the British for not firmly stating their claims when the treaty was signed.

By the time Macfie visited in September of 1859, tempers had cooled considerably, mostly because of Baynes' calm reaction to the crisis. But Baynes was severely tried, not only by Harney's rash and ill-considered statements and actions, but also by the continuing opinions and actions of James Douglas. Douglas was unhappy over the way in which he had been brushed aside, and outraged by what he saw as Baynes' knuckling under to the Americans, a response—or more precisely, a lack of response—he saw as the equivalent of the British inaction that forced the HBC off the Columbia River. Douglas wrote angrily to Baynes, declaring that he knew more about the character of the Americans than did either Baynes or Hornby. This kowtowing to them would lose the islands, while Douglas' policy would have kept them for the British.

Baynes was not about to change his mind. The fate of the San Juans would be determined by a rational process of diplomacy between the two nations, not by ill-considered conflict. The recommendations of the boundary commission would go to the governments of Britain and the United States for a final decision.

The Grand Pacificator Moves

Messages travelled exceedingly slowly between the northwest coast of North America and the capital cities of the United States and Great Britain. Eventually, though, the news of the doings on San Juan Island arrived in Washington and London. Communication between the two capitals could take place much faster, just a matter of 10 days or so by steamship across the Atlantic. Even so, the traditional pace of diplomatic exchanges was turtlelike compared to the speed of events on the west coast.

General Harney told various people that he was acting with the knowledge and under the command of his superiors in New York and Washington. Such was not the case. His letter recounting his initial landing of troops, penned in mid-July, finally reached General Winfield Scott in early September and was instantly forwarded to the president of the United States, James Buchanan. Neither could quite believe what they had read.

The acting Secretary of War immediately drafted a letter to Harney, on behalf of President Buchanan, expressing his amazement at Harney's actions. However, he temporized, if you thought that the colonial authorities were about to take possession of the island, you were perhaps right to do what you did.

At the same time, the British ambassador to the United States read about the invasion in the newspapers. He asked the American government if the reports were true. If they were, was the government behind the landing of troops? He had already asked the Americans to speed up the process of settling the boundary. Why had he received no answer?

The Secretary of State reassured the ambassador: the government had told Harney to maintain a joint occupation. The ambassador was not completely satisfied by the answer. For a week and more, the two exchanged notes and relayed each country's official position. The more information the ambassador got, the more unhappy he became: events on the coast seemed markedly different than the official American policy of peace. What was going on? Then came the news of the landing of the additional American troops. Now President Buchanan himself was newly alarmed. Was war about to break out?

Buchanan sent a telegram to General Winfield Scott, the

Grand Old Man and commanding general of the American army. Hero of the Mexican-American War, military tactician, one-time candidate for the presidency of the United States, he had had enough of political interference in his command. Scott now just wanted to be left alone to run the army. To that end, he had moved his headquarters to New York, as distant as he could reasonably get from Washington. Seventy-three years old, his six-foot-five frame now somewhat stooped and burdened by his weight of more than 300 pounds, plagued by gout and injuries suffered in a riding accident, he was still an impressive figure. His reputation for diplomacy and restraint in inflammatory situations, which had earned him the sobriquet of the Great Pacificator (though he was also called Old Fuss and Feathers), and his undoubted intelligence would serve him and the United States well in the coming months.

Scott had run into Harney at an earlier stage of both their careers. In overall charge of American troops in the Mexican-American War, Scott had been dismayed by Harney's impetuous acts and refusal to obey the commands of his superiors. He had relieved Harney of his command. American army affairs at the time were also political, and expansionist president and Democrat James Polk had supported Harney and reinstated him. A 19th-century biography of Harney characterized Scott's actions as flagrant and petty persecution, though Harney's subsequent conduct suggests that Scott had the right of the matter. Buchanan and Scott were certain that

Harney would not be bound by any commands sent from New York; Scott must go to the west coast himself.

He took ship for Panama, crossed the isthmus by land and continued up the west coast, arriving at Fort Vancouver in late October. The trip had done Scott little good. His various aches and infirmities, plus his dislike of unnecessary movement—unless accomplished on the back of a horse—made him unwilling to disembark or even leave his cabin, where he ate heartily in the fine and heavy style he preferred.

Scott summoned Harney to the fort and had him come aboard ship. The dislike between the two men was palpable, but with his backer no longer in office and a new president in Washington, Harney knew he must answer to the commanding general. Scott asked Harney for an explanation of his actions. He heard Harney's half-truths and self-justifications with increasing disbelief and revoked most of Harney's orders. He also disapproved strongly of Harney's actions when he was in command on the mainland. Pickett was also at Fort Vancouver and was summoned to meet Scott; Scott dressed him down for what he considered amateur and unmilitary conduct.

Harney and Pickett dismissed from his company, Scott continued on to Olympia, the capital of the Washington Territory, at the foot of Puget Sound. But he did not call on the territorial governor, Richard Gholson, who was again miffed, this time because he had not received the courtesy of a visit. Scott was making few friends, but he was not concerned. He had come to the west coast to sort out a mess, and he was intent on doing so. He used his time aboard ship to write to James Douglas, communicating with the British civil rather than the military authority in the region, an act that must have further infuriated Gholson. Why do we not, Scott asked, enforce a joint military occupation—coming in late to something Douglas had wanted all along. Scott also sent his proposal off to Washington.

By now, however, Douglas had reconsidered. There were too many American troops on the ground, and he did not want to tie up British naval personnel in a joint occupation. He realized now more than ever that the military could be the problem, not the solution, and he characterized Harney and Pickett as the villains of the whole affair. The Americans had hundreds and perhaps thousands more men readily available to them on the west coast, while Britain had already mustered all the force it could on the Pacific. And much of that force was naval, not army, ill-suited to any sort of land-based confrontation.

Could we not, he asked Scott, remove all our military personnel and continue with a joint civil occupation? The question completed the circle for Douglas, for the San Juan difficulties had begun with two magistrates, an ill-defined double civil system that had precipitated the trouble. He must in any case, he told the general, seek approval from London for any plan for joint control. With communications so slow, that would take upwards of two months.

The American government dispatched the Great Pacificator, General Winfield Scott, to the region to try to ratchet down the tension and solve the Pig War crisis.

Scott seemed to be coming to common ground with Douglas. Harney, however, was still at odds with his commander. The British, he wrote to Scott, were duplicitous, had sinister designs on the islands and were never to be trusted. Scott waved his concerns aside. In his view, the British wanted peace and a continuation of business as usual until the boundary question was resolved.

Scott did tell Douglas, however, that he could not withdraw the American troops. Local authorities, as Douglas knew, had already tried a joint civil occupation, with these lamentable results. And who, he asked Douglas, returning to the original stated reason for the dispatch of American troops, would protect the settlers from the Natives if the military withdrew? No, all he could allow would be a joint military occupation. Each nation could place 100 men on the island. The commander of each unit would act as the civil magistrate for cases involving the citizens of his respective nation. Americans would not interfere with British citizens, and the British would not interfere with Americans.

There were, of course, gaping holes in Scott's suggestion of non-interference, since American settlers were well ensconced in what Douglas had considered a British farm, and they were unlikely to move on. But Douglas understood that withdrawal of all American troops would bring about a loss of face for the perceived slight to the nation's honour. He agreed to compromise. Instead of a full withdrawal, he suggested after consulting with Rear Admiral Baynes, the reinforcements that had come with Captain Casey should be withdrawn, along with the heavy guns and artillery. In return, he would withdraw some of his naval forces and promise not to land any troops. And he would send dispatches to

London, asking for agreement to the idea of a joint military occupation, with each side fielding 100 troops.

Douglas had one more request. In a private communication, his aide suggested in the most diplomatic terms he could find that Captain Pickett be removed from the scene, since his presence would serve only to exacerbate any hard feelings that remained. "You will smile at this and with no doubt with reason too, but the words [spoken by Pickett] stand recorded nevertheless, and have never been revoked by word . . . his excellency has been informed (but with what shadow of truth he cannot judge) that Captain Pickett is of somewhat hasty temperament and somewhat punctilious and exacting." Should Pickett be removed, it would "ensure a continuation of perfect harmony and tranquility."

As unimpressed with Pickett as he was dismayed by Harney, Scott agreed on all counts. He ordered the American troops to stop work on their fortifications and sent dispatches to all the American commanders in the region, declaring that since the San Juans were in dispute, American and British citizens had equal rights on the islands. And he replied to Douglas via an aide that Pickett would be leaving San Juan for Fort Bellingham, his place to be taken by Captain Lewis Hunt. Another low achiever at West Point, but more calm and diplomatic than Pickett, Hunt made little secret of his feelings about Harney, writing to family members and, more seriously, anonymously to various newspapers, to derogate his commanding officer.

Tribune departed, leaving *Satellite* in Griffin Bay. On November 5, Scott ordered all but one company under Hunt's command withdrawn from the island. Two days later, Scott arrived at Griffin Bay aboard *Massachusetts*. It had been an eventful passage. The famed west-coast fog of late autumn had enveloped *Massachusetts*, and the ship had run aground on a nearby spit, held fast for 24 hours as the tide rose and fell and the fog slowly lifted. Scott still stayed aboard, rather than reviewing the troops on land, citing seasickness—or perhaps it was indigestion from his latest heavy meal. If his refusal to disembark was eccentricity, it was at least consistent. Since Scott would not come ashore, the men on land honoured him with a 13-gun salute.

The men in camp were delighted with the order to withdraw. Summer's pleasant weather had given way to the cold winds, heavy fog and slashing rains of November. "A black cloud came down," wrote Peck on November 7 of one particularly ugly day, "bringing a severe windstorm which raged furiously. There was great rejoicing at the orders to suspend work on the fort. Tools were collected quicker than ever on a former occasion."

It was not all joy and celebration. Never are military men promoted faster or awarded more honours than in actual combat, and Peck lamented that they would get no credit for anything they had done on San Juan Island. The withdrawal, he suggested, came as a direct result of Harney's precipitate actions; Harney had few supporters among the men he commanded.

Preparations for departure continued over the next several days, with Peck looking forward to being better housed at their next location. "The remainder of the detachment [other than the three men who were out surveying] preparing to leave this gay and festive [place]. As soon as may be, and if this cold weather continues, we will be much better with something more substantial for protection than cotton cloth [the tents that housed the men]. It was with considerable difficulty we kept alive in our tent last night."

The work went slowly. Peck and his companions were still on San Juan a week later. Tempers began to flare. Two men started an argument about "quartermaster's animals" and became so angry that they loaded their pistols and were about to shoot it out when their superior officer threatened them with arrest and court martial—probably much to their relief.

Another week of dull and dreary weather followed. A corporal was arrested for firing his pistol near the camp but was released. Hunt doled out punishment to the entire group, ordering them to build an addition to his quarters, a penance not well received by the men. Thanksgiving Day came and went without departure ("I shall have to remember that I dined from bean soup and pork, while they [his family at home in Connecticut] will undoubtedly fare quite sumptuously on turkey, chicken, etc."). The American soldiers were increasingly unruly. So aggrieved were they by their instructions to improve the captain's house that they intentionally shingled it badly, ensuring that the roof would leak in the winter rains. The weather improved, but the men's state of mind did not. Peck and several companions were given passes to leave the camp and went out to kill some game birds or animals, because "thus far, nothing has lost its life by our deadly aim."

They were waiting for transport, but *Massachusetts* was still under General Scott's command. As it travelled through the waters of Puget Sound, Scott wrote letters to most of the parties in the dispute, including Douglas, Gholson and Harney, laying out his decisions and the reasons for them. Gholson reacted angrily; he had been left out of the decision making even though he was governor of the territory that he claimed included the San Juans. And he was most unhappy that he and the rest of the civil government in the region were to have no right to deal in any way with British subjects on San Juan.

Harney was instructed to put no impediments in the way of the resolution of the dispute, as defined by Scott and Douglas, and was told to withdraw many of the troops and send Pickett back to Fort Bellingham. Captain Hunt would be Pickett's replacement. Scott transferred to another American ship, then tried to resolve the problem of Harney. He wrote again to Harney, urging him to step down voluntarily as commander of the Department of Oregon and assume command of the Department of the West in St. Louis, Missouri. After all, Harney had previously asked to be posted to St. Louis to be closer to his family. Harney was still extremely resentful of the way he had been treated. When Scott added that he was sure that the British would demand Harney's departure, Harney refused the reassignment.

The Washington Territory press was happy to weigh in with its opinions. The Olympia *Pioneer and Democrat* was fervently on Harney's side and detested Scott's actions. They could be seen, the editorial writer said, as "almost *treacherous* concessions to the importunate demands of the English." Scott, to that point, could have been proud of his 20 years of service in battle and out, defending the rights of the United States. He was now 72. "Would to God that . . . time had spared a seventy-third year, a year that witnessed the only deed which deserves the censure and condemnation of his countrymen," the editorialist opined. Perhaps we might pardon this horrendous mistake, "an error unpardonable in one in the enjoyment of more youthful age or mental vigor." An interesting reaction, considering that just over a month earlier, on October 28, the same paper had reported the appointment of the venerable general with praise for his "good judgment and wise counsel."

Massachusetts finally arrived at Griffin Bay to take off the troops on November 28. Almost everyone got drunk the previous night, with the recalcitrant ex-sergeant the most intoxicated of all. The departure wrote the final chapter to the saga of the sergeant. Peck wrote, "Many of the men came aboard drunk, and of course, our foolish Sergeant among them. He must abuse and insult Lieutenant Robert, and is now under arrest and will undoubtedly be tried by Court Martial on our arrival at Vancouver."

So, Peck continued, "After three months and eight days duty and excitement in the teeth of the British Lion, we leave with few laurels added to those already decorating our fair brows." Nonetheless, he declared, it had been pleasant duty, and they had done as good work as could be done under the circumstances.

With the departure of Scott, the placating of Douglas, the successful diplomacy of Baynes and the reassignment of the new troops on San Juan, the dispute had been cooled off. But the flame of anger had not been extinguished, especially on the American side.

8

The Occupation

SAN JUAN VILLAGE WAS IN an uproar. Shacks lined the muddy street, whisky flowed at all hours of the day and night, soldiers reeled from seller to seller then staggered home again to their camp late at night. Native people came and went from the area around the sound and from Vancouver Island, and the American settlers carried pistols and took advantage of the unregulated trade in alcohol.

Such were the results for the Americans of the declaration of a joint military occupation of San Juan Island. Civilian traders bitterly resented any interference in their business by the military authorities. Cautioned, arrested or occasionally thrown off the island, they were wont to appeal to the civil authorities in Washington Territory, who were equally resentful of the new military authority.

As early as mid-November, the settlers had drafted resolutions expressing their dismay at recent events. San Juan Island was part of Washington Territory, they declared, treaty and Scott be damned, and any title claimed by Britain was futile and preposterous. Harney was able, distinguished and popular, and his actions were judged "wise, prudent, conciliatory, truly patriotic" and the readiest solution to the problem. Their support was not surprising, of course, for their land claims would be proved out only if the island was declared American. The territorial legislature and Gholson issued a resolution praising Harney and, by implication, condemning Scott.

Pickett's replacement, Captain Lewis Hunt, suspected that Harney would replace him again with Pickett the second that Scott's back was turned. Hunt tried to deal with the chaos that was San Juan village by sending soldiers to find goods stolen from the camp—but the townies threw the soldiers out of a whisky seller's and into the mud. Saloon owners complained to Harney that Hunt was trying to put them out of business; Harney told Hunt to leave the saloon keepers alone. Hunt sent Harney testimony from the more responsible of the settlers, describing the reprobates, and said he had tried to get the civil authorities, in the person of magistrate Henry Crosbie, to enforce the law.

But Harney had no intention of listening to Hunt. In

April, he ordered Pickett and his men back to San Juan; Hunt and his men were commanded to leave the island and return to Fort Steilacoom. Harney once more was rejecting any notion that the British had any rights whatsoever on San Juan. Pickett returned to the island on April 30.

The chaos around the American military camp continued. "Ever since the knowledge of the joint occupancy," wrote Pickett on June 1, 1860, "the desperados of all countries have fought hither. It has become a depot for murderers, robbers, whisky sellers—in a word, all refugees from justice. Openly and boldly they've come and there's no civil law over them." The announcement that British authorities would deal with British citizens, American authorities with Americans, resulted in some miscreants announcing they were British if they were detained by the Americans, American if they were detained by the British.

On the other end of the island, though, life was much calmer. Rear Admiral Baynes had continued to oppose a joint military occupation, believing such an occupation would suggest British citizens needed military protection from the Americans. In his view, they did not. But when orders finally arrived from London early in 1860, he had been overruled: a force of 100 Royal Engineers, members of the British Royal Marine Light Infantry, was to be moved to the island from New Westminster.

The Americans had no problems deciding where to locate their camp for the joint occupation: they chose to

The two sides agreed to a joint occupation of the island until the territorial dispute was resolved. American Camp, near the original sheep farm, housed American soldiers throughout the occupation.
US NATIONAL PARK SERVICE

occupy Pickett's camp, the farthest distant from Belle Vue headquarters and therefore the one least likely to cause problems for the farm. But the British had conducted their side of the dispute from water and now had to find a site for their military camp. Seeking information on likely sites, they questioned boundary commissioner James Prevost, whose endeavours over the past few years had included a survey of the island. Prevost outlined seven possible sites. Baynes chose a location well distant from the American camp, some 12 miles by trail on Garrison Bay on the north end of the island. One of Prevost's officers had described the Garrison Bay site as "well-sheltered [with] a good supply of

113

water and grass, and . . . capable of affording maneuvering ground for any number of men that are likely to be required in that locality." By siting the British marines far from the American campsite and San Juan village, Baynes hoped to avoid, as much as possible, contact and quarrels with the American soldiers and, more likely, the American settlers, who he knew were still spoiling for a fight.

On March 21, 87 men and officers landed at the site to begin clearing the land and erecting barracks, houses and farm buildings. Sergeant William Joy described their arrival:

> Landed in a bay completely land-locked, our Camping Ground being on a shell bank—the accumulation of years, evidently, as it averaged ten feet high, from thirty-five to forty feet through, by 120 yards long. It was the work of Indians, as they live very much on a shell-fish called "Clams", and of course deposit the shells just outside their huts, hence the bank I mentioned. The brush wood grew quite down to the water's edge, in the rear the forest was growing in undisturbed tranquility, yellow Pine, White Pine, cedar, Alder and Willows in the low flat ground are the general features of the North end of the island.

Captain George Bazalgette was placed in charge of the camp. Born to a Nova Scotia family in the late 1820s, Bazalgette was trained in England and commissioned as a second lieutenant in the Royal Navy in 1847. After fighting in the Opium War in China, he arrived in British Columbia in 1858, as part of the contingent of marines and Royal Engineers sent to protect British interests as the gold rush developed. He must have found the west coast a placid place after his experiences in China, and San Juan promised to be even sleepier. His orders for duty on the island were precise:

> The object of placing you there is for the protection of British interests, and to form a joint military occupation with the troops of the United States. As the sovereignty of the island is still in dispute between the two Governments, you will on no account whatever interfere with the citizens of the United States, but should any offense be committed by such citizens which you may think it advisable to notice you will send a report of it immediately to Captain Hunt, or officer commanding the U.S. troops. American citizens have equal rights with British subjects on the island. Should the officer commanding the U.S. troops bring to your notice offenses committed by any of Her Majesty's subjects you will use your best judgment in dealing with the case, and I authorize you, if you deem it necessary, to send them off the island by the first opportunity. If any doubts arise as to the nationality of an offender you will not [decide] in the case before you have consulted with the U.S. commanding officer, and not even then unless your opinions coincide. You will place yourself in frank and free communication with the commanding officer of the U.S. troops, bearing in mind how essential it is for the public service that the most perfect and cordial understanding should exist between you.

Baynes requested a whaleboat for the camp, two cooking stoves and a quantity of lumber and other building materials. At Garrison Bay, work began on a 40-by-20-foot commissary, and Bazalgette requisitioned supplies, including "84 tin pannikins, 36 tin plates, 3 'dishes', 10 camp kettles, 18 lanterns, 1 measures set, and a small quantity of stationery." Work also proceeded on the barracks and cookhouses that would be needed for the following winter. In the meantime, the men were housed in 13 bell tents, the officers in two larger marquee tents. In June, Baynes visited the camp and asked for an extra clothing allowance for the men, since the hard work of clearing the trees and brush had worn out the clothing they had. He also requested the extra pay usually granted to those serving in the colonies, but the Admiralty was stingy: they would get the extra, it dictated, only if they did work above and beyond the usual.

Civilians who dropped by from Victoria reported on the air of general contentment at the camp. Anglican bishop George Hills visited English Camp in mid-October 1860. He found the picturesque and serene location was well supplied with fruits and vegetables from the garden the marines had planted. "Wild fowl is abundant. There were hanging up in the larder of the kitchen geese, ducks, the common wild duck & canvas back, teal & wild muscovy. A fine wild goose can be had for half a dollar if you buy one, later they will be made much cheaper." Deer could also be shot for a fine venison dinner.

The engineers on the site drew up plans for camp buildings, including a 56-bed barracks, a non-commissioned officers' bedroom and mess room, a privates' mess room and a kitchen for the men. There would also be a hospital with room for six men. A blockhouse built by the shore would guard against attack and also serve to house prisoners, whether from among their own men or from the civilian population of the island. It was tough work excavating through rock and stone for the buildings, but the result was attractive. The buildings were painted white with yellow trim, the paint made using lime from the lime kilns on the island.

Everyone involved in the decision to have a joint military occupation thought the occupation would be short-lived, no longer necessary once Britain and the United States resolved the boundary dispute. Britain suggested that arbiters should be called in and pressed its claims as well for compensation for property taken over from the HBC when the United States took possession of Fort Vancouver on the Columbia River. Diplomatic notes went back and forth across the Atlantic.

But the polite discussions of diplomacy were soon overtaken by more urgent events. In 1861, war broke out between the northern and southern states, primarily over the issues of slavery and states' rights. For four years, as Union armies faced the southern Confederacy on the battlefields, the American government had no time for less critical matters. The question of ownership of a small cluster of islands far from the battles of the Civil War fell off the American horizon, and the occupation continued in an increasingly courteous manner.

In 1861, soon after the Civil War began, Bishop Hills was back visiting English Camp. Captain Bazalgette reported to him the state of affairs in American Camp. Bazalgette had become good friends with Pickett, who, now the immediate confrontations were over, had transformed himself from aggressive soldier to courteous diplomat, eager to avoid trouble. The Civil War had little impact at English Camp, but things were different at American Camp. Wrote Hills:

> Captain Pickett is a Southerner, others of his officers are Northerners. They had a feud the other day but this is made up again. They expect the Dissolution of the Union—know not what will become of them. One of their troubles is arrears of pay and inability to get even U.S. treasury Bills cashed. No one has confidence enough or patriotism enough to venture to cash even the Government Bills upon Washington. The same fate awaited the U.S. Revenue Ship Massachusetts the other day at their own coal mine Bellingham Bay. The Colliery people refused to supply the coals except for cash and refused a Government Bill.

As battles raged in the eastern United States, military authorities there needed all the troops they could get to fight on the Union side. Early in 1861, the American troops on San Juan were ordered to abandon their island camp and travel east. That order was soon reversed, but it was a last straw for Pickett. He could no longer in conscience serve in the Union army; his heart was with the Confederacy. He resigned his military post. Still conscientious, he waited for a replacement commander to arrive and then headed home to fight for the south.

Later in 1861, relations between the United States and Britain soured as the Americans on the Union side accused Britain of giving aid and comfort to the Confederacy. In November, two representatives of the Confederacy sailed for London on a British merchant ship to ask the British and French governments to recognize the 11 secessionist states as a separate country. An American navy ship stopped the British ship at sea, and the two men were removed. The British viewed the Union actions as the illegal boarding of a non-combatant ship and put their forces on full alert. Some in the Union wanted to declare war on Britain. The Confederacy was not averse to such a move; it would reduce military pressure on the secessionist south and might bring about recognition of the region as an independent country. Antagonism between Britain and the United States grew. The dispute simmered on but did not boil over, despite anger on both sides. It was perhaps as well that the Union government had no time to spare for thoughts of the San Juans. And the region was never of much interest to the Colonial Office in London, much to the dismay of James Douglas and other officials in Victoria.

With little official interest in affairs on the islands, the occupation dragged on. By all accounts, it was a relatively pleasant time, despite drunkenness, fights and the aggravations caused by whisky sellers. Arguments between military authorities and civil authorities and settlers over who had jurisdiction on the island were mostly confined to harsh words. Officers from the rival camps raced their horses against each other, attended religious services together and generally found more in common with each other than they did with the settlers from their own country. Soldiers from both camps and settlers celebrated Queen Victoria's birthday, May 24, at English Camp, and the Fourth of July at American Camp.

As the months and then the years passed with nothing much happening at the camps, excursionists continued to visit from Victoria. One such trip allowed visitors to celebrate Queen Victoria's birthday with the troops on San Juan. "After a pleasant run of two hours the party reached the beautiful and sequestered camp of the British garrison," the *Colonist* reported on May 26, 1866. The officer in command took the ladies ashore in his own boat, while the rest followed in the ship's boats. On shore, the groups wandered into the woods looking for shady spots where they could relax. Scarcely had they done so when the officers announced that field sports were about to begin.

The sports began at one o'clock, with many of the passengers eager to compete. The jumping and racing were excellent, and "the wheel-barrow race blindfolded evoked intense amusement, the men rushed about in all directions and several of them disappeared, barrow and all, over the embankment. Only one of the number approached anywhere near the goal. The two sack races and the bobbing for rolls also created great laughter."

According to the *Colonist*, "As the steamer was about to get under weigh the last game which consisted of walking a greasy pole extending 15 feet from the end of the wharf at the extremity of which was a stick three feet high with a bunch of evergreens, worth $3 to the person who could reach it came off. From the deck of the vessel the excursionists witnessed several men who attempted the perilous journey take an involuntary header into the briny deep." The group then sang "God Save the Queen," some semi-official words were spoken and the visitors returned to their ship, with the reporter noting the neatness, cleanliness and general good order of the camp. The group danced on deck all the way home to Victoria.

Life on the southern end of the island, around the village of San Juan and the American military camp, was less idyllic. The settlers and civil authorities had no more liking for American military authority than they had had for the British. Many of those who came to the island after the American soldiers landed were attracted by the fact that no taxes or customs duties could be collected.

Until the day he left the island, Pickett battled the civilians over whisky sales and dissolute behavior, especially since drunkenness and desertion were not uncommon among the American soldiers. Pickett departed, and Captain Lyman Bissell took over in February of 1862. "I found the island infested with thieves and vagabonds of no particular nationality," Bissell reported. He tried to enforce the laws he thought were in effect, but the settlers resisted, and a number of the merchants passed a resolution completely rejecting military authority. Bissell was greatly disappointed in the response of the brigadier commanding the US Department of the Pacific. Tell the settlers that military authorities will not interfere with them in any way, the brigadier said, and that the duly elected or appointed civil authority will be in charge.

This response virtually destroyed any authority Bissell might have had, and he reacted angrily, trying to describe to his superior officer the state of affairs on the island and the character of the men who had penned the resolution:

> Mr. Higgins is postmaster, but lives by dealing out his poisonous liquor to my men, thereby destroying them for usefulness, Mr. Offutt, the secretary of the meeting, at one time kept a low whisky ranch in the town and dealt out his vile stuff to soldiers and Indians, but being detected in selling liquor to the Indians last fall he left the island, and was not a resident . . . Mr. Hibbard has a lime kiln on the island and keeps liquor for sale . . . to Indians and to the soldiers of the British camp. Last fall he tried to create a disturbance between the officers of the two camps by writing a dictatorial letter to Captain Bazalgette, because Captain Bazalgette ordered two of his men out of his camp that went there for the purpose of selling liquor to his men.

The offences continued through the 1860s, with a variety of whisky sales to the Natives, drunkenness, thieving, and the occasional kidnapping, assault and murder. On occasion, questions arose over which lands and resources were American and which were British. The marines stationed at English Camp had quarried limestone near present-day Roche Harbor and made whitewash. The Americans tried to do the same and were stopped by two of the marines, who told them the area was within the British reserve. The Americans protested. Under Pickett, the military reserves under the control of each country had been delineated, and the British had kept the Roche Harbor area.

In other incidents, some American settlers dressed down both American and British military authorities, telling them to mind their own business. Captain Thomas Grey took over from Bissell and continued to battle with the liquor dealers and other malcontents, including rowdy settlers. When postmaster Higgins built a fence across the road between American Camp and the HBC wharf, Grey ordered him to tear it down. Higgins refused. After a stint in the guardhouse, Higgins was released and ordered to leave the island. Higgins again refused. Finally, after Grey's threats of jail and hard labour failed to convince the postmaster, Grey's men thrust Higgins into a canoe manned by Indians and three armed soldiers and removed him from the island.

Higgins filed charges of malicious trespass against Grey

The Americans and British dug in for what turned out to be a long occupation. Here, British officers relax at English Camp.
US NATIONAL PARK SERVICE

and his adjutant, and a warrant was issued for their arrest. Eventually, after a lower-court decision against the commander, the case was thrown out of court with a ruling that the island was under military rule. A later case of murder was resolved when the military on the island simply turned the case over to the civil jurisdiction.

As the decade rolled on, the British forces dwindled. Desertions, departures, drownings and other deaths reduced their numbers, and no new reinforcements arrived. One of Bazalgette's marines even compounded his sin of deserting by enlisting with the American forces. By the end of 1866, only 47 officers and men manned their posts at English Camp. On July 24, 1867, Bazalgette, who had been away from England for 16 years, was replaced by Captain W.A. Delacombe, who arrived with his family. The men built new quarters for the Delacombes and the new second-in-command, First Lieutenant A.A. Beardon, and began work on a new formal garden. The marines also were equipped with new Enfield rifles. A few months later, the American soldiers kept pace with new Springfield rifles.

Life continued on at the camp much as life in other British military encampments. The men ate their rations of biscuits and meat, vegetables and sugar, chocolate and tea, spirits and wine and beer, and spices and bread, supplemented by wild game and fish. They tended the large vegetable garden, looked after the flowers in the formal circular garden with its walks between the main camp and the officers' quarters, and raised and lowered the flag. They drilled daily, built new structures and maintained the existing buildings at the camp. Meanwhile, the camp commander rode his own horse, sometimes in the company of the commander of American Camp. There are records of horse races between the two.

Late 1869 marked a full decade of joint military occupation. On New Year's Day, 1871, at English Camp, the soldiers welcomed visitors. "The soldiers of the garrison . . . decorated the barracks with evergreen, holly, the Union Jack and other national insignia, and on Monday evening received a large number of the residents of the island and entertained them with a supper and a ball." It would be the last full year of the occupation at English Camp.

CHAPTER

9

Resolution

THE AMERICAN CIVIL WAR ENDED in 1865, but the San Juans still did not seem to be on the minds of anyone in Washington, DC, or London. The legislature of Washington Territory wanted an end to the joint claims and the military occupation and petitioned the federal government to move ahead. But they were not heeded.

The islands were still small potatoes in the large hill of American and British irritants. During the war, Confederate ships were allowed the freedom of British ports around the world. This gave them bases from which to attack Union merchant ships. Some of these Confederate ships had had British crews, and British companies had supplied much of the armament used by the Confederate army during the war. If it weren't for Britain, ran the Union argument, the war would have been over much sooner, with much less loss of life and destruction of property.

At least one American senator had a solution: either the British would pay for the damage caused by the Confederate ships, or they would have to cede all of Canada to the United States. The idea was a non-starter. There was some appetite for war with Britain, but not enough, since British loans were helping restart the American economy. Finally, in 1869, the British and Americans agreed that it was time to settle the question of the boundary, as well as several other claims and counterclaims between them arising from actions in the Civil War.

The two bickering nations signed the Treaty of Washington on May 8, 1871. The treaty settled the claims arising from the loss of merchant shipping during the Civil War, agreed on the appointment of a commission to settle differences over fisheries off the northeast coast, and declared that the question of jurisdiction over the San Juans would be submitted for arbitration by the Emperor of Germany.

The treaty was unpopular in Canada, newly unified as a nation in 1867, for it seemed to cede too much to the United States. In fact, though, secret negotiations with the British gave Canada some redress for losses suffered.

Kaiser Wilhelm, selected as the arbitrator, in turn handed the job over to three commissioners: a professor at the

University of Berlin, a councillor from the Imperial High Court of Commerce of Germany and the vice-president of the High Court of Germany. The three argued for more than a year before voting two to one to award all the San Juan Islands to the United States, with the international boundary running through Haro Strait. On October 21, 1872, the Kaiser made his public declaration of the outcome, and the dispute was officially over. By that time, the map of the northwest had changed once more. British Columbia had officially entered Confederation as a province in 1871, and was now part of the new nation, though one still tied to the apron strings of the British Empire, with Britain still able to regulate Canada's foreign affairs.

With the boundary finally decided, it remained only for the British troops to depart. On November 21, HMS *Scout* weighed anchor at Garrison Bay, and the evacuation began. The stores, ammunition, government property and supplies were taken aboard. At 11 a.m., the troops were lined up, inspected and marched down to the ship. *Scout*'s captain declared, "Marines, you are a credit to your country."

The *Colonist* reported, "The crowd of Citizens who assembled to witness the evacuation and take leave of their old friends, many of whom have been here for many years, and one ever since the detachment was first formed, gave them three hearty cheers, which were returned by the soldiers in a lusty manner."

The barracks and commandant's residence were handed

The dispute resolved, the occupation over, the British forces left San Juan Island forever, their legacy the sturdily built camp structures and a formal garden. The flag was lowered for the last time and the flagpole chopped down, leading to one final squabble between the sides. US NATIONAL PARK SERVICE

over to the American forces at 2 p.m. "The flagstaff, from which the British ensign had floated for thirteen years, was cut down, a portion divided among the men and a long piece brought back to the Dockyard as a souvenir." The Americans had wanted to run their flag up the pole but instead affixed the Stars and Stripes to a telegraph pole near the wharf, and soldiers and settlers cheered lustily as it was raised.

The good feelings of the bittersweet departure did not touch everyone. Early the next month, a US marshal complained to the Puget Sound newspaper that the flagpole was cut down because "Captain Catron, of the Marine Service" declared, "No damned Yankee flag should ever float from that staff." But a correspondent from the

Daily British Colonist declared the marshal had been hoaxed, because there was no captain called Catron on the ship, nor anyone else by that name—a perhaps disingenuous response, since *Scout*'s captain was R.P. Cator.

There were more serious difficulties ahead. The treaty did not spell out what would happen to the properties claimed by British citizens on San Juan, and some hungry companies had no intention of respecting even the American settlers on the island. Early in January, the Northern Pacific Railway Company claimed that since their charter allowed them to take up all unsurveyed lands around Puget Sound, they would be claiming all the land in the San Juan Islands, since the islands had never been officially surveyed. The Puget Sound newspaper commentator raised an eyebrow at this, suggesting that "the Company will find it a difficult task to wrench the islands from the grasp of the hardy pioneers who hold them—and would hold them if necessary by armed force."

The matter of British citizens' claims on the island raised hackles. The governor of Washington State declared that these people would have to declare their allegiance to the United States if they wished to continue on the land, since American law did not permit non-citizens to pre-empt or own former government land.

Member of British Columbia's legislative assembly, former newspaper editor and future premier John Robson waxed eloquent on the unfairness of such a stand and on the fact that the treaty had not protected the Britishers. "If an Indian potatoepatch or fishing station were to be protected, no doubt British statesmen would have looked after their interests," he declared. The BC government sent notice of the problem to the Governor General in Ottawa and hoped for resolution soon, since a number of Victorians held interests on the San Juans.

Several weeks later, the Washington State governor told a reporter that almost all the British on the islands had signified their intent to become Americans, so there would be no further problem. And, he said, the railway company could not take any land where pre-emptions had been filed before February 10, 1872—excluding almost all settled land on the islands. Surveys were expected to be made on the island later in 1873. The HBC moved its sheep and cattle off the island—and presumably the remaining pigs went too.

What would be done with English Camp? The captain of one of the Royal Navy ships sent a telegram to England (the trans-Atlantic telegraph had been completed in 1864) but had heard nothing by the time he was told that Americans were planning on taking over the camp. He turned the site and the buildings over to the commanding officer at American Camp. On July 17, 1874, the remaining American troops left the island.

The land at English Camp was homesteaded by American settlers from 1875 on. In 1894, the commanding officer's house burned down. Abandoned for many years, it had recently been renovated by new owners as a summer residence.

CHAPTER

10

Happy and
Not-So-Happy Endings

THE QUESTION OF WHICH COUNTRY owned the San Juans
was deeply important to those who lived in this tiny cor-
ner of North America, but it raised scarcely a ripple in
the affairs of the greater world. Similarly, the events of the
Pig War were but a paragraph in the stories of many of those
who had the biggest roles in the events.

Lyman Cutlar, whose shooting of the pig provided the
catalyst for the "war," left the islands and settled on the
Washington Territory mainland, in Snohomish or Skagit
county. He died on April 27, 1874, leaving behind possessions
that included the double-barrelled shotgun of fancy English
manufacture that supposedly was used to shoot the pig,
though Cutlar himself termed it a rifle, and some say it was

an entirely different gun. He also left his house, some saws, three books, a stove, a grinding stone, 30,000 shingles, three steers, three cows and a yearling steer—but apparently no pig—with a total value of just under $500. The bill for burial, payable to the Bellingham Coal Company, included alcohol, lumber for a coffin, six yards of muslin, five yards of alpaca, four and five-eighths yards of ribbon and a dozen screws. It is quite possible that he did not rest in peace, despite the expenditures. His coffin may have been transferred to a second cemetery when the first was developed, or it may have washed out to sea.

William Selby Harney decided after all to take up a position as commander of the American army in the Midwest, in Missouri, and was there when the Civil War broke out. Ironically, his decision then to exercise diplomacy and not fight ended his career. Allied by marriage with a Confederate brigadier general, he pledged not to interfere with the Missouri State Guard as long as its members did not openly challenge the northern forces. The decision was not well-regarded by the Union army, and he was recalled to Washington and relieved of command. He lived in Missouri and Mississippi until his death in Florida in 1899. He was buried with full military honours.

Though George Pickett was personally opposed to slavery—a major issue in the Civil War—he remained loyal to his native state of Virginia, part of the secessionist south. He became a brigadier general in the Confederate army;

his career there was marked by "Pickett's Charge" in the Battle of Gettysburg, in which he commanded, "Up men and to your posts! Don't forget today that you are from Old Virginia!" The charge became a bloodbath and resulted in half his men being injured or killed. The battle has been called the bloodiest ever fought on American soil.

A later defeat under his command was one of the last Civil War battles; at the time he was two miles away at a fish bake. Orders were sent relieving him of his post, but in the chaos of the last days of the war, they may never have reached him. He surrendered to the Union troops and was paroled, but fled, in a great irony, to Canada. He sought amnesty, but was not pardoned until a year before his death in 1875.

William Peck, who recorded life in American Camp, left the Army Corps of Engineers in 1862, disabled by an accident when a mule kicked him at Fort Steilacoom. He worked on coastal defences in Maine as a civilian during the Civil War, then continued on at harbour works on the east coast for the rest of his working life.

General Winfield Scott was already over 70 when he arrived off the San Juan Islands; the incident occupies just a few lines in his military biography. He was the general-in-chief of the American Army when the Civil War began, but was too old and infirm to go into battle himself and too large to mount his horse. Though he, like Pickett, was Virginia-born, his loyalty was to the north. His carefully thought out strategy for Union troops was much ridiculed by the non-military, but it formed the basis for Union success in the war. His girth and age also occasioned much ridicule, but he served his country with honour and diplomacy until his retirement in 1861. He died in 1866. Said to have been uttered by a soldier under his command, the phrase "Great Scott!" may be a lasting legacy of this distinguished general.

Calm and cool-headed, Captain Phipps Hornby continued in the Royal Navy, serving in the Mediterranean and then as the officer in command of the English Channel fleet. It was said he was the most able commander on the Royal Navy active list. He became admiral of the fleet, then the principal naval aide-de-camp to Queen Victoria. He died in 1895.

Rear Admiral R. Lambert Baynes, who deserved much of the credit for defusing the confrontation, remained as commander of the fleet in the Pacific until 1860. He was knighted in 1869 and became an admiral in the Royal Navy in 1865. He died in 1869.

And what of James Douglas, the former HBC man who wanted to protect the company's interests throughout the northwest, the man who resented the incursions of the Americans, and the man who as governor of Vancouver Island and British Columbia ordered British marines to land on San Juan Island? His reaction to the arbiters' decision was characteristic: he could not believe that the British case had been well presented, for otherwise the Germans could not have reached such an "unjust decision." He tried to react with equanimity, although he was not reconciled to one more defeat at the hands of the Americans. In a letter to his daughter Martha, he wrote, "We have lost the stakes and must just take it easy . . . The island of San Juan is gone at last. I cannot trust myself to speak about it and will be silent."

By the time the decision was announced, Douglas no longer held any position of power in the northwest. His term as governor of Vancouver Island expired in 1863. At the request of the British colonial secretary, who stressed that the move was not a reflection on Douglas but a step toward more responsible government in British Columbia, he stepped down as governor of both colonies in 1864. He was knighted on his retirement and toured around Europe in 1864–65. He died in Victoria in 1877, at the age of 73, probably of a heart attack.

Douglas had served the HBC well and profitably. He ensured that law and order prevailed despite the chaos of the gold rush, and he oversaw the building of the first roads through the interior of British Columbia. Though he was often excoriated for his arrogance and aloofness, he treated Native peoples well, given the prevailing attitudes of the day, and perhaps because of his own mixed-race heritage, he was accepting of other races.

The legacy of James Douglas is large: his actions may well have preserved British Columbia as part of the British Empire and kept it from becoming an American state.

The English Camp blockhouse still stands, though its log foundations have been rebuilt several times, as time and tides wear away at the blockhouse base. LIBRARY OF CONGRESS HABS WASH, 28-FRIHA, 1-1

San Juan Island Today

The events and legends of the Pig War are commemorated at the San Juan Island National Historic Park, created in 1967. The park includes both American and English camps, with the park headquarters at American Camp open year-round. Displays at the sites include artifacts from several thousand years of Native occupation, as well as of the Pig War era. A number of the original buildings, suitably restored, are still standing at the English Camp site; only the officers' quarters remain at American Camp. A formal English garden created by English Camp's second commanding officer has also been restored.

What of the island today? American officials claimed—and British officials feared—that the island would become a strategic military site, but the Pig War was the last of the coastal hostilities between British and Americans. By the time the controversy was settled, Canada had become a nation from the Atlantic to the Pacific, and American expansionist fervour had declined. No military base was ever established on the island.

Today, the San Juans are quiet agricultural, tourist and logging areas. Perhaps they are even home to a rambunctious, rooting Berkshire boar.

Bibliography

Books

Adams, John. *Old Square-Toes and His Lady: The Life of James and Amelia Douglas.* Victoria: Horsdal & Schubart, 2001.

Gough, Barry M. *The Royal Navy and the Northwest Coast of North America, 1810–1914.* Vancouver: University of British Columbia Press, 1971.

Macfie, Matthew. *Vancouver Island and British Columbia: Their History, Resources, and Prospects.* London: Longman, Green, 1865.

Peck, William. *The Pig War: The Journal of William A. Peck Jr.* Medford, Oregon: The Webb Research Group, 1993.

Richardson, David. *Pig War Islands.* Eastsound: Orcas Publishing Company, 1971.

Vouri, Michael. *Outpost of Empire: The Royal Marines and the Joint Occupation of San Juan Island.* Seattle: Northwest Interpretive Association, 2004.

———. *The Pig War: Standoff at Griffin Bay.* San Juan Island: Griffin Bay Bookstore, 2006.

Websites

British Colonist. University of Victoria Digital collections. http://britishcolonist.ca/. This and other British Columbia newspapers are also available on microfilm at the British Columbia Archives, as are many documents relating to the era.

Colonial Despatches. http://bcgenesis.uvic.ca/index.htm. More and
more resources that relate to the colonial era in British Columbia
in general and to the Pig War specifically are now online. In 2010,
documents to the end of 1858 had been scanned into the database;
more will be added as time and resources allow.

Historic Newspapers in Washington. http://www.sos.wa.gov/history/
newspapers.aspx. This website includes Washington State
newspapers from the mid-century.

San Juan Island National Historic Park. http://www.nps.gov/sajh/index.
htm; Erwin N. Thompson, *Historic Resource Study: San Juan Island
NHP*, 1972, http://www.nps.gov/history/history/online_books/
sajh1/hrs.pdf.

Index

141

Acknowledgements

Anyone writing about the Pig War owes a considerable debt to authors of earlier studies and books, and I gratefully acknowledge the great assistance these sources have been in the writing of this book. Many of the quotes from those involved in the events of 1843–72 come from these previously published sources. Most useful were Erwin N. Thompson's 1972 *Historic Resource Study: San Juan Island NHP*, a fine treatment of the war, its origins and events, which also includes illustrations, maps and a detailed inventory and history of the structures on San Juan; and two books by Mike Vouri, chief of interpretation and historian at San Juan Island National Historic Park: *The Pig War: Standoff at Griffin Bay* and *Outpost of Empire: The Royal Marines and the Joint Occupation of San Juan Island*. Both these books contain fine research and a wealth of detail on the subject. Mr. Vouri also kindly provided photographs for the book and answers to several thorny questions about the time of the Pig War. William Peck's journal, published as *The Pig War: The Journal of William A. Peck Jr.*, is a good first-person account of time spent on San Juan.

Heritage House publisher Rodger Touchie has long been fascinated by the Pig War. I thank him and managing editor Vivian Sinclair for giving me the chance to write about this byway of Pacific Northwest history. My thanks, too, to editor Lesley Reynolds for her highly professional work on this book.

About the Author

Author Rosemary Neering has been writing about the Pacific Northwest for more than three decades. A freelance writer for much of that time, she is the author of many books on the area, including *Down the Road: Journeys through Small-Town British Columbia*; *Wild West Women: Travellers, Adventurers and Rebels*; and *A Traveller's Guide to Historic British Columbia*. She is fascinated by the offbeat and lesser-known stories of the region. She lives in Victoria with her partner Joe Thompson and her cat, but makes frequent forays into the backwoods.